Finches

2nd Edition

by Nikki Moustaki

Finches For Dummies®, 2nd Edition

Published by: **John Wiley & Sons, Inc.**, 111 River Street, Hoboken, NJ 07030-5774, www.wiley.com

Copyright © 2022 by John Wiley & Sons, Inc., Hoboken, New Jersey

Published simultaneously in Canada

For general information on our other products and services, please contact our Customer Care Department within the U.S. at 877-762-2974, outside the U.S. at 317-572-3993, or fax 317-572-4002. For technical support, please visit https://hub.wiley.com/community/support/dummies.

Wiley publishes in a variety of print and electronic formats and by print-on-demand. Some material included with standard print versions of this book may not be included in e-books or in print-on-demand. If this book refers to media such as a CD or DVD that is not included in the version you purchased, you may download this material at http://booksupport.wiley.com. For more information about Wiley products, visit www.wiley.com.

Library of Congress Control Number: 2021944962

ISBN 978-1-119-75531-9 (pbk); ISBN 978-1-119-75532-6 (ebk); ISBN 978-1-119-75393-3 (ebk)

SKY10030265_093021

Table of Contents

PART 3: TRAINING AND BREEDING YOUR FINCHES

Introduction

Finches are charming companions, adding a little bit of life to an empty corner of any home. Whether you plan on having just a pair, or would like a whole aviary full, finches offer a glimpse into the natural world, and give owners hours of watching and listening pleasure. They are easy to care for, relatively quiet, and some are prettier than a rainbow. What more could you ask for in a birdy friend?

About This Book

Finches For Dummies is a book I wrote for people interested in finches. Maybe you just bought finches or a canary and need the essential scoop on getting set up as well as general care information. Or, you may already have finches and you need a refresher on the best way to take care of your companions or want to understand them better. Perhaps you're ready for a new feathered friend but aren't sure if finches are right for you and your family. If any of the above describes you, keep on readin'.

As you read, keep an eye out for text in *italics,* which indicates a new term and a nearby definition — no need to spend time hunting through a glossary. And `monofont` points out web addresses for additional information worth checking out. You'll also run into a few sidebars (the occasional gray box); although the information in the sidebars is good, it's not essential to the discussion at hand, so skip 'em if you want to.

Foolish Assumptions

In writing *Finches For Dummies*, I made some assumptions about my readers:

>> You're one of the millions of people who wants finches or who has a family member who wants one (or more) and you've come to this book to learn about their care.

>> You already have a canary or some finches, maybe a pair or a flock, and you want to brush up on finch care and learn a few things that you don't already know.

>> Maybe you're a volunteer at a bird shelter or rescue and you want to be able to educate your adopters more thoroughly.

>> Perhaps you want to begin breeding these popular little birds and want some information on how to make that process go smoothly.

Whatever the case, whether you're a newbie or a seasoned finch guardian, there's something in this book for you.

Icons Used in This Book

While reading *Finches For Dummies,* be on the lookout for these icons, sprinkled here and there:

TIP

This icon flags tips and tricks that will help you be the best finch friend you can be.

REMEMBER

This icon points out information that's so important you'll want to be sure to remember it.

WARNING

This icon highlights information on things that could harm you or your finches.

TECHNICAL STUFF

This icon flags information that you can use to impress your friends with your amazing bird knowledge, but it isn't absolutely necessary, so don't feel the need to memorize it.

Beyond the Book

You can find a little more helpful finches-related information on `https://www.dummies.com`, where you can peruse this book's Cheat Sheet. To get this handy resource, go to the website and type *Finches For Dummies Cheat Sheet* in the Search box.

Where to Go from Here

Finches For Dummies is a reference, so you don't have to read it in order from start to finish. Begin with Chapter 5 if you need basic setup information, flip to Chapter 9 if you're thinking about breeding finches, or head to Chapter 2 if you're still on the fence about adding finches to your family. (Although those of you who prefer to start at the beginning and read until you reach the back cover are welcome to do so. I'll never tell.)

1

Introducing Finches

Chapter **1**

Finches: More Than Just Pretty, Chatty Birds

The term *finch* is actually a very broad term, encompassing hundreds of species and subspecies, from canaries to sparrows. In general, finches are small songbirds that come in an amazing variety of colors, shapes, and sizes. They all have short, cone-shaped bills adapted to the type of food they typically eat. All finches are seed eaters, but most will eat other vegetation and insects as well.

Finches have been kept as companions for hundreds of years. The Chinese and Japanese have been breeding finches since the 1600s — for example, the society finch (also known as the Bengalese finch) is not found in the wild because it was developed (domesticated) by humans, much as breeds of dogs were. It's also one of the most widely kept finches today. The canary is the oldest domesticated bird, having been bred in captivity for many centuries, and, like dogs, bred for certain traits, such as color, feather type, or song (its ancestor, the serin finch, is still found in the wild in the Canary Islands). Finches that have a long history with humans do very well as companion birds. They tend to be hardier and less skittish than other types of birds, who haven't been around the bird scene for as long.

In the following sections, I show you what makes a finch a finch.

Where Finches Come From

Because they comprise such a large group, finches are found in every corner of the world. Even the Galapagos Islands are home to 13 species of finches, all of which were studied by famed British naturalist, Charles Darwin. The finch was one of the animals used in Darwin's theory of natural selection, which posits that ecological and social pressures can actually change an animal's physiology.

WARNING

If you're reading this in the United States, you can only keep finches that aren't native to North America. This goes for all birds, actually. If a bird is native to North America, housing it is illegal unless you have a permit or are a licensed bird rescuer. Birds that fall into this category include the American goldfinch, the cardinal, and the pine siskin, among others.

Most of the companion finches available for purchase are native to other countries but were bred in captivity where you live. As of 1992, it is illegal to import birds from other countries under the Wild Bird Conservation Act.

The Life of a Wild Finch

Some finches are very social by nature. They live and forage in flocks, sometimes numbering into the hundreds. This is why people rarely keep finches alone — with the exception of the canary, who likes company only during breeding season, and otherwise does not prefer a cagemate. Most finches do not do well unless they are in a pair or a flock. Wild finches feed mostly on grass and weed seeds, and eat insects as well, usually during the breeding season, and feed them to their young. They sleep in soft nests at night, even when not breeding. As a small, defenseless prey bird, they rely heavily on their senses and their quickness for survival.

Finches will pair off within a flock. These are generally mating pairs, although not always. Occasionally, two males — or two females — will choose to become companions. Pairings do not always last for life, but while they are together, pair companions stay very close to one another within the flock. They forage together, groom each other, and nest together at night.

Most finches are monogamous, but some, like the orange weaver, keep a harem and will chase off other males who try to invade their territory. Other finches, such as the whydah, are considered *parasitic,* laying their eggs in other birds' nests so that those birds can take over incubation and rearing duties. They rely on these other birds the way parasites rely on other animals to survive.

The Many Species of Finches

One of the more fascinating things about finches is their seeming endless variety. They range from very delicate to very hardy birds, in all colors of the rainbow. Some are drab and others are exceptionally vivid. Many species are *dimorphic,* which means that you can distinguish the gender of the bird just by looking at it. Others are *monomorphic,* which means that you can't visually distinguish the genders of the birds.

TECHNICAL STUFF

All finches are scientifically grouped under the order *Passeriformes.* Passerines (which is what birds in the *Passeriformes* order are called) comprise more than half of the bird species in the world, with nearly 5,400 members. Not all Passerines are finches, but all finches are Passerines.

Though no one expects you to become an *ornithologist* (someone who studies birds), in order to provide a good home for your companion finches, it can be helpful to understand where your bird is classified in the scheme of things. Here are the four different groups of finches:

>> **Fringillidae:** The more than 200 (some sources say 227) members of this group are often called the "true" finches. This family includes the canaries, chaffinches, some siskins, rosefinches, goldfinches, and bullfinches. These finches are adapted to crush seeds and, as a result, they have strong skulls and jaws. These finches are found on all continents.

>> **Passeridae:** This group of around 40 finches includes sparrows and snowfinches. Formerly found only in Europe and the surrounding areas, these finches have now been introduced to habitats all over the world. Two types of Passeridae are commonly found in the United States, including the house sparrow. As a group, they are hardy and gregarious songbirds.

>> **Estrildidae:** Included in this group of around 140 birds are some the most popular companion finches, including grass finches, parrot finches, waxbills, society finches, greenfinches, serins, firefinches, firetails, quailfinches, Gouldian finches, mannikins, nuns, munias, Java sparrows, cordon-bleu finches, cut throats, and zebra finches. The majority of finches in this group are from a temperate climate, preferring warm weather. They tend to be flocking birds and are all seed-eaters.

>> **Ploceidae:** This group has approximately 120 members, including the whydahs (also called widowbirds) and weavers (also called bishops). They are found primarily in Africa and India and can be more aggressive in their response to other birds than some of the more commonly kept species.

One of the longest domesticated and most popular varieties of finch is the well-known canary (see Figure 1-1). Canaries come in a variety of colors, from bright yellow, like the famous Tweety Bird, to brown, gray, orange, white, and *variegated* (having either regular or uneven dark markings). Canaries are delicate birds, originally from the Canary Islands, and have been a popular companion in Europe since the 16th century, perhaps even earlier.

FIGURE 1-1:
Canaries are among the most popular types of finch.

Most people buy a canary for his beautiful song. The males are the singers of the species, and they're generally the gender that you'll keep if you want to hear singing in your home. The females can make great companions too, but they won't launch into song the way a male will.

TECHNICAL STUFF

The canary's song depends largely on the type of canary that you choose. Some canaries sing a variety of songs, whereas others are trained only to sing in a certain manner. Yes, canaries have to be trained to sing. Many breeders keep an "expert" singer, a canary with a particularly masterful song, in a cage within earshot of young males. The youngsters will learn from this maestro and, hopefully, pick up the essentials of beautiful singing. Some interesting research has shown that birds can actually learn songs when they are developing inside the egg! Don't worry if you don't have a master singer to teach the young males their trade; CDs and audio files of canary songs work just as well (you can buy these online or play them for free on YouTube).

Size differences

Finches can vary in size from about 3 inches in length to about 8 inches in length. Some finches are very tiny, such as the gold-breasted waxbill, measuring in at under 3 inches. The whydah, who is only 5 inches in length, has a tail that can reach 15 inches long during breeding season.

I SEE YOUR TRUE COLORS SHINING THROUGH . . .

TIP

Some canaries, like the red factor canary shown in the figure below, turn various shades of red and orange if they're fed a special color food or water additive made for red factor canaries only. It's the only way for a red factor canary to achieve colors ranging from magenta to bright orange to strawberry red.

Isselee / 123 RF

Don't feed your other types of canaries the color food, as their color will not change because of it. Only the red factor has the genetic predisposition to show what it eats though its feathers, much like flamingos and roseate spoonbills, which pick up their pink coloration from the crustaceans that they eat. Color feeding is usually done during a molt, when new feathers are growing in. If you don't want to color feed with commercially prepared products, you can feed your red factor canary beets, cherries, red and orange peppers, carrots, cayenne pepper, paprika, and other red and orange fruits and veggies to help maintain their color.

Temperament differences

In terms of companion quality, most finches are the same. Some are more skittish than others, but for the most part, they all make wonderful companions. Some can be more demanding in terms of nutritional needs or housing, and others are far easier, such as the zebra, society, or owl finch.

Finches aren't aggressive toward children or other pets. The reverse is far more likely to be true. However, some species of finches are aggressive toward other species of finches, and all varieties of finches will have more of a tendency toward aggression during the breeding season.

TIP

If you're going to keep a large *aviary* (a home for birds that's large enough for an adult human to walk into), and you wish to have more than one species represented, do some research ahead of time to find out which species will be most likely to get along. For example, weavers are quite aggressive and the males will hurt, or even kill, other species and other males of their own species. Society finches, on the other hand, get along so well that more than a dozen of them will try to crunch themselves into one nest to sleep for the night.

Most of the time, finches will shy away from human contact. Taming a finch to appreciate human contact is possible, but that depends a great deal upon the individual finch and will usually require more patience and effort than most bird guardians are willing to devote. Remember that your companion finch is a very delicate creature and easily frightened. Too sudden a shock or fright can be fatal to your little friend. However, you can find many adorable videos online of hand-tamed finches.

The finch lifespan

Most finches live to be between four and ten years old, with some variations among species. Some have been reported living 15 years or more. Although it's very rare, finch guardians have also reported that their finches have lived up to 27 years! Now that's a well-cared-for finch!

Anatomy of a Finch

Knowing the parts of your finch is a good idea so that you can describe a problem to an avian veterinarian or an online finch group if you have to do so. Knowing the different parts of your finches is also a good idea if you're going to breed or show your birds. This way you can speak like an expert with other hobbyists. Here are the parts of your finch you'll want to be familiar with (see Figure 1-2 for an illustration).

>> **Crown:** The *crown* is simply the top of the head. It's an important word to know in finch-speak because many finches are identified by the color of the crown.

>> **Nares:** The *nares* (nostrils) are at the top of the beak and may not be visible because they're often covered by fine feathers.

>> **Beak:** The upper and lower mandibles make up the finch's beak. In the case of a finch, it's short, wide, and rather triangular in shape. This is for crushing the tiny hard seeds that make up most of your finch's diet. The beak is made from the same tough material that makes your fingernails.

>> **Ear and ear coverts:** Your finch has tiny flat holes for ears, and they're covered by *coverts,* or tiny flaps of skin bearing feathers, which protect them from the wind when flying. This is why your finch's ears are difficult to see.

>> **Eyes:** The finch's eyes are on either side of its head so that it can see a wider area than you can see with your forward-facing eyes. A finch needs a wider range of vision because it's a prey animal and needs to be on the alert for predators. Finches, like many birds, have a third eyelid called a *nictitating membrane,* a thin semitransparent lid that washes the eye like a squeegee and closes for protection.

>> **Throat:** The throat is just beneath the beak and extends to the breast. Many finch species are identified partially by the color of the plumage at the throat.

>> **Nape:** The nape is the back of the neck.

>> **Shoulder:** The shoulder is at the top of the wing, nearest the finch's back.

>> **Breast:** The breast is just below the throat.

>> **Foot:** Everything that most people think of as a bird's leg is actually a bird's foot. That's why the "knee" appears to bend the wrong way — what you may be thinking of as the bird's knee is actually the heel. As for toes, finches have three front toes and one toe that grips to the rear.

>> **Vent:** The vent is where your finch eliminates waste (and also lays eggs if it is a hen). In a human, this would be a combined anus and urethra. Birds do not urinate.

>> **Primary feathers:** Finches have ten long primary wing feathers that aid in flight.

>> **Secondary feathers:** The secondary feathers on the wing occur after the primary feathers; they're smaller and closer to the body than the primaries are.

>> **Rump:** The rump is beneath the primary flight feathers on the finch's lower back.

>> **Mantle:** The *mantle* is the bird's back.

>> **Crop:** The *crop* is a sac-like organ that's kind of like a "first stomach." It's where the food goes immediately after being swallowed and is located at the breast. You can see the crop very well in baby birds.

>> **Gizzard:** The *gizzard* is like a "second stomach" that grinds food to digest it.

>> **Syrinx:** The syrinx is equivalent to vocal chords in humans. It allows finches to sing when air is pushed through it.

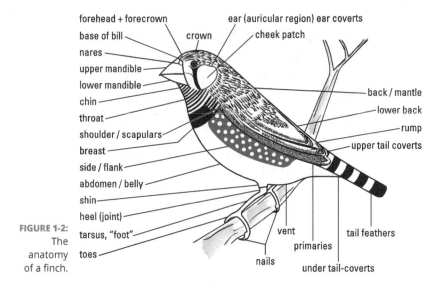

forehead + forecrown
base of bill
nares
upper mandible
lower mandible
chin
throat
shoulder / scapulars
breast
side / flank
abdomen / belly
shin
heel (joint)
tarsus, "foot"
toes

crown

ear (auricular region) ear coverts
cheek patch

back / mantle
lower back
rump
upper tail coverts

vent
primaries
nails
under tail-coverts
tail feathers

FIGURE 1-2:
The anatomy of a finch.

Chapter **2**

Are Finches Your Perfect Companions?

I f you're trying to decide whether to bring finches into your home, you've come to the right chapter. But don't worry — even if you already have finches, this chapter has something for you. Here you figure out what to expect from your finches (from their seemingly endless energy to the messes they make) and what your finches expect from you. I walk you through the challenges posed by children and other animal companions. I also give you information on owning more than one finch and fill you in on breeding finches (and what you should consider before you do so).

Knowing What to Expect from Finches

Finches and canaries have the reputation of being a small bird that you place in a small cage, much like a goldfish on display in a bowl. Many people believe that one of these smaller birds will live for only two to three years at the most and that there is little point in becoming deeply attached to them because the birds won't live very long. Nothing could be further from the truth!

Finches make wonderful companions, and if you take good care of them, you'll be able to enjoy your finches for between 4 and 10 years, perhaps even more. Most finches are curious, amazingly intelligent, and develop very distinctive personalities. You won't want to miss out on the very real pleasure of getting to know and love them.

In the following sections, I fill you in on some of the traits you should expect from finches.

Activity

Finches are very busy and active little birds. They spend a great deal of their day flying from perch to perch and interacting with their companions. They play with simple toys, usually preferring something shiny or something they can preen. They also build nests, both for sleeping and for breeding. Finches are much simpler to keep than parrots, which need a lot of out-of-the-cage time and handling. Some people do allow their companion finches to fly around their home, but this isn't the norm due to the many dangers in an average household, ranging from other pets to open windows.

Noise

Finches do sing, although they aren't nearly as noisy as the more raucous and larger species of birds, especially parrots. Most people greatly enjoy finches' soft twittering, cheeps, and peeps. Usually, the male finch is the one who sings — and nearly always to his mate or potential mate. The more finches you have, the more noise there will be, though the noise from even a large flock of finches rarely annoys their guardian or the neighbors.

TECHNICAL STUFF

A charming revelation about finches has come out of the scientific community (though they probably didn't mean it to be charming): Finches dream about singing. Studies on zebra finches have shown that they're so devoted to learning their song that they even dream about it.

Enjoyment

You can look forward to many hours of enjoyment watching your finches go about their daily lives. If you pay attention to what they're doing, you'll probably find that they are a nice diversion from your phone or tablet screen.

Finches aren't considered hands-on companions, though some people do manage to tame their finches or handfeed babies so that they're tame. These tame finches are few and far between, but they're not a myth — "taming" is generally done out of necessity, because a baby has been abandoned or fallen from the nest.

TAMING A FINCH: NOT FOR THE IMPATIENT

If you have the time, you may want to undertake the difficult and delicate task of attempting to tame your finch. There is no joy quite like having your tiny feathered friend perch on your shoulder and snuggle trustingly up to your neck, but be aware that coaxing a finch to this degree of trust takes a tremendous amount of time and patience, and most finches will simply never accept a close human bond. A simple search on YouTube will show you not only a plethora of adorable hand-tamed finch videos, but also some how-to videos to help you on your quest.

If you're determined to finger-tame your finch, you'll want to adopt or purchase a bird that is just old enough to leave the nest, or tame one of the babies you've bred from your parent finches.

(continued)

(continued)

First, get the bird comfortable with your presence. Talk to her soothingly and move slowly near the cage. Offer millet spray though the cage bars and talk to her as she eats it. Develop a noise that's all your own, such as a distinctive whistle or clicking or kissing sound, and do it every time you enter the house and/or approach the cage. All these things will start making the bird more comfortable with your presence.

After she's comfortable with you, open the door to the cage (only if the cage is in a safe, bird-proofed room — do not move the cage to a new location or you're going to have to start over). Allow the finch to come out on her own. Sit still, make your distinctive noise, and hold some millet spray. If you've succeeded in gaining her trust, she may come to you for a treat. Don't push it or put too much pressure on the finch you're attempting to tame. If she doesn't come out the first time, just keep trying each day until she does. It may happen that the bird will never come to you. It's all up to her — you can't force contact.

When you want her to return to her cage, put something in it that she absolutely loves, like egg food. If she doesn't return, you may have to use a bird net to gently capture her and put her back. Or, wait until dusk or turn out the lights in the room and she may go back on her own, but this isn't always the case. If not, look for where she has gone to *roost* (sleep) and gently grasp her and put her back in the cage.

Taming finches is easier when you have several finches or a flock inside a walk-in aviary or habitat. Sitting quietly with them in their space holding food that they love will entice them to land on your hands to eat.

Mess

Your finch will always require a good deal of housecleaning. Finches scatter loose feathers, bird seed, soft food, and water, along with anything else they are in regular contact with, which is why their cages should be located on a floor that you can clean easily, such as terrazzo, tile, or wood.

If your finches fly free for occasional periods, you'll have to clean some droppings from furnishings and carpets also. Chances are that you won't object seriously to this if you're enchanted by birds, but your housemates, family, and guests may object to the mess. Keeping a bird from being messy is completely impossible, of course, so if you're around someone who seriously objects to ongoing mess, you may want to consider a different type of animal companion or confine free-flying to one bird-proofed room.

Knowing What Your Finches Expect from You

Your finches won't expect much from you except proper care and attention so that they can live a happy and healthy life, so you need to know what your finches require in order to help them do exactly that.

Proper care for finches consists of more than just putting seed and water in a cage. Your finches rely on you for all of their needs: proper housing, nutrition, and safety. You're responsible for every aspect of their lives. In the following sections, I let you know what your finches need from you, but here's a list of basics to get you started:

>> **A clean cage:** Clean the bottom of your finches' cage every day if possible, or at least every other day. Once a week, you need to clean the cage and the surrounding area more thoroughly. I discuss cleaning more in depth in Chapter 6.

>> **Water:** Offer your finches fresh water twice a day if possible (at least once a day, minimum). Throw out the water from the day before (or the hours before) and replace it so that your finches always have a fresh water supply.

>> **Food:** Offer and change fresh foods once a day, and not just seeds. Finches need a considerable quantity of fresh vegetables, greens, live food, and egg food, in addition to bird seed. Just as with water, if your finch hasn't eaten all the food you gave him the day before, throw out the old food and replace it with new. (*Note:* You should change the water twice a day, but you only need to add or change the food once a day.) I discuss more about proper finch diet in Chapter 6.

>> **Attention to his health:** Your finches can't just fly to the vet's office when they feel under the weather. You need to watch your birds closely for signs of illness, and take them to the veterinarian if you suspect something is wrong or if your birds have had an accident of some sort.

>> **A safe home:** When you bring a finch into your home, you need to make sure it's a safe place for your bird to live. (See Chapter 5 for more information on finch-proofing your home.) Also make sure that your finch's cage is away from drafts and that the room where he lives doesn't get too cold or too warm.

In addition to these basics of bird care, your finch needs other things from you, covered in the following sections.

A good home

A good home for finches provides them with everything they need to be healthy and long-lived:

>> **They need as large a cage as your wallet and space can afford.** I discuss cage types in Chapter 5.

>> **They need access to direct sunlight or to be provided with bird-specific full-spectrum lighting.** If the cage is in direct sunlight, the finches should have a shady, cooler place where they can retreat.

>> **They need to live in moderate temperatures, ideally somewhere between 70° and 80° F (21° to 26° C).** Some finches that aren't from the tropics can handle winter weather if they're acclimated to it. Be sure to allow them to adjust gradually to the falling temperatures.

>> **Finches also need cleanliness.** You need to clean your finch's cage frequently. Bird waste is fairly inoffensive and easily cleaned when it's relatively fresh, but it dries every bit as hard as concrete in a very short time, and then powders to a fine dust that is dangerous for humans (and finches) to breathe for extended periods.

The longer you wait to clean your finch's cage, the more time you'll need to spend cleaning it. Most bird-care experts recommend cleaning a cage at least once a week, but giving it a quick once-over daily is easier and far less trouble.

Routine

In the wild, finches schedule their days around the sun. They understand the seasons and how to behave when water or food is scarce or plentiful. In nature, the same events happen day after day, year after year, and these birds are programmed to go with the flow.

Your finches are pretty much the same birds with the same programming, but their lives are far different. Even if your finches' lives are cushy, the lack of routine can become stressful. Finches are genetically programmed to do certain things at certain times of the day; for example, they want to eat in the morning, when they're hungriest. You can snack all night if you want, but finches have an innate understanding that if they're snacking at midnight and making noise, they're fair game for a lurking predator.

TIP

VACATIONING WITHOUT YOUR FINCHES

Finches are tiny creatures with a very fast metabolism. Your finches could literally die of hunger or thirst in the course of a single day, so you'll need to make careful and reliable arrangements to care for your birds if you're away from home for more than a day. Don't try to load up on food and water inside the cage thinking that you can leave for a week that way. You may come home to a disaster.

Though you can travel with your finches, travel can be difficult and disorienting for them. In addition, these small birds are extremely susceptible to illness when stressed, so exposure to drafts or cold can literally be fatal. Try to leave your bird home with a reliable bird-sitter, if possible.

TIP

Create a routine and try to stick with it. Your finches should know exactly when you're going to feed them, when you're going to clean the cage, and when it's time for bed. If you keep a routine with your finches, they may eventually alert *you* when you've missed a step. If your life is hectic, just do the best you can.

Deciding Whether a Finch Is Right for You

Adopting or purchasing any animal companion is a serious responsibility. By keeping any creature in captivity, you become responsible for its health and happiness for the duration of its natural lifespan. In the case of finches, that lifespan could be fairly short, so making every day a good one for these little birds is important.

Before you consider bringing a finch into your home, ask yourself whether your lifestyle is one that can provide a happy life and home for your companion birds. Also, think about whether you can commit to whatever changes will be necessary to provide a good environment for your new friends for as long as they live.

In the following sections, I offer some questions to ask yourself before you consider owning a finch.

Will finches fit into your family?

You'll need to make certain that the other people who share your house and your life also share your enthusiasm for your feathered pals. Have a family meeting and discuss your plans to have and/or breed finches. Though finches are much less trouble than many other types of birds, you and your housemates will have to put up with a certain amount of mess and noise, and a complaining or unhappy family member can take a lot of the joy out of the experience.

HOUSEGUESTS

You have to ask all your houseguests, whether they're just visiting for an afternoon or staying for a month, to respect your finches and their housing. If the person doesn't know much about birds, and if his or her only bird contact has been with a parakeet or another hands-on bird, he or she may not understand why your finches won't come out to perch on a finger. Be sure to explain that finches are different from other birds.

If you're having a party, you can post a note on your finches' housing, or simply move them from the room. If you think your party may become especially rowdy, be sure to move your finches to a room that's off-limits to the partygoers.

REMEMBER

Though some finches can be tamed enough to accept human handling, taming a finch takes a very long time and a great deal of work. The vast majority of finches, even those bred in captivity, are going to be frightened if someone tries to touch them. Touching an untamed finch unless it's absolutely necessary is unkind, and if the behavior is prolonged or rough, it can be terrifying and even deadly. Everyone in the house should understand this and put the finches' needs above their own.

Do you have any smokers in the house?

WARNING

Tobacco smoking (and other kinds of smoking) absolutely must not be permitted near your finches. Finches have very delicate respiratory systems, and smoke is deadly to them. Everyone in the house must also know not to spray any household cleansers or air fresheners, or light candles near the birds for the same reason.

Before you bring a finch into the home, make sure everyone you live with is okay with these restrictions. You want to get their agreement *before* you own finches — otherwise, you're not being fair to your future feathered friend.

Is your home also home to children?

Very young children or unruly older children can be a danger to your finches. Inappropriate handling, feeding of unhealthy items, and excessive noise can stress a finch, or even kill it. Children should be taught not to handle the cage or the finches, not to put anything into the cage, and to use "indoor voices" around the birds.

However, when a child is ready, he can learn a tremendous amount from finches about the natural world and how to care for small animals. A finch is certainly never a danger to a child — it's usually the other way around.

REMEMBER

Curious children should be taught to enjoy finches at a safe distance (see Figure 2-1). Attempts to handle the birds should be restricted to a need-only basis and done only by an adult or older child. Your house rules must also be made extremely clear, even for kids who spend the night.

TIP

To ensure that smaller children don't invade your finches' space, use tape to create a box-shaped area around the cage and instruct the children not to cross the tape. This will give them the ability to watch the birds, but will restrict them from putting fingers into the cage, opening the doors, or placing unhealthy food items inside.

TIP

Here are some basic ground rules to share with your children when you first bring your finches home:

>> **Move slowly.** Birds are frightened by quick movements. Explain to the child that the birds won't hurt her and that it's important to remain calm, no matter what happens.

>> **Speak softly.** A screaming child is terrifying to finches. Instruct your child to use a soft, soothing voice when talking to the birds.

>> **Don't stick fingers in the cage.** Teach your child not to stick his fingers or other objects into the cage. A child should not feed the finch without supervision, either, because the child may feed the birds something they shouldn't have.

>> **Never shake, hit, or rattle the cage.** Finches are going to be only as entertaining as they can be. Your child may not understand this and may try to get the finches to do something more interesting. Explain to the child that the finches becomes frightened when their home is rattled.

>> **Never take the finches outside.** Your child may want to show off her birds to friends, and though that's a valid response, many dangers lurk outside, including the birds flying away.

FIGURE 2-1:
An adult must always supervise a child around finches.

jackf / 123 RF

Do you have other pets?

Dogs and cats definitely consider finches to be tasty snacks. Even other birds pose a threat. A cross-species friendship is rare, and a finch doesn't have any defenses against a more powerful bird. Even a very frightened or aggressive finch is unlikely to have a painful bite, except to another finch.

REMEMBER

If you have other animals, your finches' cage should be inaccessible to them, and your finches should never be allowed to fly free when the other animals are loose, such as dogs or cats. Snakes will also prey on finches and will find it easy to break into most finch cages. Also, standing water, such as in a fish tank, toilet bowl, or deep dog dish can pose a drowning threat to your finches.

You may see videos online of adorable finch/cat or finch/dog relationships. These are few and far between. For every cute video like this, there are thousands of stories of predator pets eating or killing finches. If you look online, you'll find a lot of "cat TV" videos of finches meant to entertain cats with one of their favorite snacks!

How Many Finches Are Right for You?

Most finches are social birds, and they need interaction with other finches to be happy and well-adjusted. Consider purchasing a pair or more of the commonly kept finches, like zebra finches, society finches, and Gouldians. Other finches, like weavers or canaries, tend to be territorial and won't appreciate other birds in the cage with them when it's not breeding season.

If you put a male and a female together, and if they're society or zebra finches or another easily bred species (see Chapter 3 for more on the various finch species), you're fairly certain to have more finches in short order. You can refrain from providing a nest, but they'll try to breed in the food dish if it suits them.

TIP

If you don't want more finches, you do have a couple of options. In the absence of a member of the opposite sex, most zebra or society finches bond reasonably quickly with a member of the same sex. All birds or all bees means no babies! Problem solved. Some species, however, are competitive, and won't like being with a member of the same gender.

TIP

Many people keep two birds, let them breed once or twice a year, and find homes for the babies when the time comes. That seems to be the easiest way to go if you're certain you're ready for the responsibility of breeding the birds and finding suitable homes for their offspring. Trust me, it's easy to start with two and shortly end up with dozens!

WARNING

If you choose to have an aviary with a number of pairs, perhaps including some of the babies you've raised yourself, be sure that they're pairing up such that they're not inbreeding. *Inbreeding* is when finches of the same family line-breed together — siblings with siblings or parents with offspring. Sometimes, a hobby breeder will *line-breed,* using parent/offspring combinations to get a certain color or pattern in the babies, but they won't continue breeding this pair once the desired results have been achieved. Inbreeding isn't a good idea, because the babies may have health problems and may be weaker than birds that weren't inbred.

TIP

To prevent inbreeding, you have to separate the babies from the parents and from each other when they become mature, which can happen quickly in finches. Zebra finches, for example, can be ready to breed at eight to ten months. Or you can choose not to provide nests and hope that the birds don't decide to breed in the food dishes or on the bottom of the cage. If they breed once accidentally, don't fret — just don't let it happen again.

REMEMBER

If you place different species in the same aviary, you'll want to be certain that they're compatible. You don't want to mix an aggressive species with a passive one. (See Chapter 3 for some information on which species tend to be more compatible or aggressive; when in doubt, talk with your avian veterinarian, other finch hobbyists, or join a few of the many hundreds of finch groups online.)

Chapter **3**

Selecting Species of Companion Finches

There are more than a thousand species of finches, though most of them are not available in the companion animal trade. Among these many different species are an absolutely marvelous number of *mutations* (including different color variations) to choose from. Different species have different personalities, too. This chapter will help you choose among some of the more commonly kept species.

Choosing Finches: Exploring Your Options

You'll be able to find some species of finches in a pet store, but you'll find more species in an all-bird store and online, and even more if you attend a bird club or bird show in your area.

The following sections illustrate only a small sampling of the available species. Dozens more are easily available as companions, and you can find even more with a little effort.

Canary

The canary may be the most well-known companion finch. They exist in a wide variety of colors and mutations, with yellow being the most common, followed by white, orange, and red.

Canaries are originally from the Canary Islands, the Azores, and other surrounding areas. The wild canary is small and drab, but possesses a beautiful song, which transfixed Spanish sailors hundreds of years ago when they colonized the islands, and they collected the birds for this reason. In Europe, the canary became a popular companion, prized for its song.

Today, the canary doesn't resemble its wild cousins due to selective breeding, a process whereby birds with certain desirable traits, such as color, type (a certain look), and song, are bred together to enhance those traits. Check out Figure 3-1 to see a crested canary bred for type.

FIGURE 3-1: This crested canary has been bred to have a mop-top of feathers on its head.

Maximilian100 / Shutterstock.com

Canaries are lively and the males will fill your house with song. Every breed of canary has a different song. In fact, there are canary song competitions! Canaries like to live alone, unlike most other finches, unless it's breeding season.

Cordon-bleu finch

Three species of cordon-bleu finch can be found in the companion bird trade: the red-cheeked cordon-bleu, the blue-capped cordon-bleu, and the blue-breasted cordon-bleu. These African waxbill finches are highly prized for their gorgeous blue plumage (See Figure 3-2). They are quite small at around 4 inches in length, and the males' plumage is brighter and more vibrant than the females'. The red-cheeked species also comes in a variety of mutations.

They can be kept with other species of peaceable finches, but can become aggressive during breeding season, especially if they are crowded. Their natural habitat tends to be hot and dry, so take care not to keep them in a cold, damp environment, which can be detrimental to their health and breeding.

FIGURE 3-2: These cordon-bleu finches are enjoying a bath outdoors.

UTOPIA88 / 123 RF

European goldfinch

These birds have been kept as pets in Europe for many hundreds of years. They are very pretty — yellow, white, and gold, with a patch of red on the face that is larger in the male than in the female. European goldfinches aren't as popular as canaries in the United States, probably because they're harder to breed, but they have a prettier and less repetitive song. Both male and female European goldfinches sing, but the females are not as intense as the males.

TIP

The European goldfinch prefers a large aviary or habitat setting and can become aggressive in breeding season. These birds are not recommended for novice owners, but after you have some experience, they can be incredibly rewarding.

Note that there is an equally beautiful American goldfinch, but it is illegal to keep this species in captivity in the United States. (This is due to the Migratory Bird Treaty Act of 1918, which bans the keeping of birds native to the U.S.)

Gouldian finch

The Lady Gouldian finch (or just *Gouldian finch*, for short) is prized mainly for its gorgeous plumage (see Figure 3-3). Originating in Australia, this bird's stunning appearance is why people fancy these tiny creatures. This finch appears as if an artist got very creative with a palate full of colors — the best specimens of these birds don't even look real until you see them hopping from perch to perch. Gouldian finches are prime examples of the miracle and beauty of nature. They're found in a variety of dramatic colors. The males of this species are brighter than the female, making them easy to tell apart at maturity.

FIGURE 3-3:
Gouldian finches are prized for their rainbow-like plumage.

kolesnikovserg / 123 RF

You'll probably find Gouldian finches with a bright red or a carrot-orange face, a green body, a blue head, a violet chest, a yellow belly, and a cobalt rump, though many mutations exist. For example, the blue Gouldian, which is primarily made up of shades of violet, blue, and white; still other mutations include shades of creams and browns.

Gouldian finches are tiny, but they make great aviary birds. They appreciate a large garden setting and add wonderful flashes of color to the foliage. As with most finches, the Gouldian is a quiet bird, hopping around and peeping. You may hear the male sing, but it is nothing like the song of a canary.

Gouldians are among the most difficult finches to breed. People who raise Gouldians usually also keep society finches in separate housing, and place the Gouldian's eggs in the society finch's nest. This ensures that the eggs and babies will get the proper care. When the babies arrive, you may be in for a shock — they're a dull grey-green and need a few months to mature to their full coloration.

Java finch

The Java finch (also called the rice finch or Java sparrow) looks painted by the hand of a master artist. This Asian finch is one of the larger finches at nearly six inches in length, and though its size may seem intimidating to smaller birds, it is actually quite peaceable and can be kept with other peaceable finches if given enough space. It can also be hand-tamed, given some patience. It tends to breed readily in warm and cool conditions.

The Java finch song is quite sweet. Only the males sing, which is a good way to tell the males and females apart. The female will be ever-so-slightly drabber than the male, but often not enough to tell them apart. They come in a variety of beautiful mutations, and because they breed readily, they are easy to acquire. (See Figure 3-4.)

WARNING

Unfortunately, the Java finch is illegal to possess in California, Florida, Georgia, Hawaii, Kentucky, Maine, Nevada, New Mexico, New Hampshire, Pennsylvania, Puerto Rico, Virgin Islands, West Virginia, and Wyoming. These beautiful birds can become a pest to crops and can possibly push out other native wildlife. You may, however, be able to obtain a permit to keep them if you live in one of these states.

FIGURE 3-4: Java finches come in a variety of mutations, including white.

Owl finch

The owl finch is a grass finch, also known as the Bicheno finch or the double-barred finch. Owl finches are a lively addition to a community aviary and a good choice if you don't have a lot of experience with birds. (See Figure 3-5.)

This bird's native habitat is Australia, particularly the woodlands, grasslands, and scrublands, though they can also be found in city parks. They travel in groups numbering 4 to 40 and are active flyers.

In terms of coloration, the owl finch can't compete with the Gouldian or even the common zebra finch, but its distinctive markings and social disposition give it a character all its own. It stands between three and four inches in length and has two distinct black bars above and below a whitish-beige chest, one bar circling the underpart of the "chin" and the other rounding the bird's underside. The wings are brown with white speckles, and the face mask is white. The beak is gray and the eye is black.

FIGURE 3-5:
Owl
finches
make great
aviary
compan-
ions.

The owl finch has one subspecies, the black-rumped owl finch, which has, as the name implies, a black rump. Because of crosses with the "normal" owl finch (which has a white rump), the rumps on some birds may be blotchy — not quite black, not quite white.

The visual difference between the sexes is so slight that even owl-finch experts have a difficult time telling the males from the females. Males are said to have thicker bands and a whiter chest, though this is not always consistent. Males do have a soft, sweet song and females do not, so separating birds and listening for the song is one way of determining sex.

Owl finches are generally good parents, but some can be a little too carefree with their sitting habits or can toss the occasional baby out of the nest. Having other similarly sized finches — such as zebra finches and society finches — nesting at the same time is convenient, because they'll generally foster the eggs or babies willingly. Owl finches who are good parents will also foster other species as well. These birds absolutely need some direct natural light or artificial bird lighting to remain healthy. They often become darker or discolored if they aren't getting enough light.

Society finch

Society finches, also called Bengalese finches, were actually created in captivity, first bred in Asia. Society finches never existed in the wild. They're domesticated, entirely "made" by humans, the way dog breeds are, and descended from a few species of finches, though no one knows for sure which ones. As a result, they're the calmest finches around humans.

TIP

A society finch could be your best bet if you're determined to tackle the difficult task of finger-taming your finches. (I don't recommend this.). Of all the varieties of finch, the society finch is the gentlest. They're pacifists by nature. If bullied by other birds, they'll generally back down. In addition, they often adopt the eggs or babies of another breeding pair and care for them as they would their own.

WARNING

Needless to say, mixing society finches with more aggressive species is not a good idea, though they do well housed with zebra finches and Gouldian finches if given enough space.

Society finches were once known as the "little brown birds," but quite a variety of mutations exist today, though colors range only from white to dark brown or cinnamon. See Figure 3-6 for an example of a society finch.

FIGURE 3-6: Society finches are more than just little brown birds.

Dorota Photography / Shutterstock.com

Spice finch

The spice finch, also known as the nutmeg mannikin, spotted munia, the scaly-breasted munia, or the scaly-breasted finch (see Figure 3-7), is a lively aviary bird that is commonly kept in captivity. This prolific Asian finch is a delight to keep and is readily available in the companion animal trade. It gets its name from the spice ships that first brought it to Europe.

The spice finch one of the quieter finches, so if you're noise-sensitive, the spice finch may be a good choice. The males have a pretty song, but the volume is low. Spice finches are from the tropics and sub-tropics, so they prefer warmer climates and will not do as well in the cold. Spice finches are *monomorphic*, which means both sexes look the same, so it can be difficult to pair them up initially, but if you hear a spice finch singing (the volume is pretty low, so you'll have to pay attention), you will know that it's a male because the hens do not sing.

FIGURE 3-7: Spice finches are pretty little birds that can be good for someone new to bird keeping.

Shubhrojyoti / Shutterstock.com

Whydah

Whydahs, native to the tropics, are glossy black and pure white, which doesn't sound very spectacular, but they're truly striking in their appearance. During the breeding season, the male grows a spectacular tail that is often twice his own body length (see Figure 3-8). When the breeding season is over, the male goes out of color and looks like an adult hen or a juvenile male.

The whydah does not raise its own young, strangely enough. The female lays her eggs in another bird's nest, and each whydah has a different "host" bird to call upon. The adoptive parents do the work for them, incubating the eggs and raising the whydah chicks, often at the expense of their own babies.

TIP

These birds are not recommended for beginners, because they're hard to raise and can be aggressive to other birds their size.

Zebra finch

Last, but definitely not least, is the zebra finch. Zebra finches are the most popular variety of companion finch kept today. In fact, they may very well be the most popular companion bird after the budgie and canary.

Native to the Australian grasslands, zebra finches are hardy little birds and easy for a novice to keep. They're also easy for the novice to breed, and rarely require human intervention in the breeding process beyond providing a nest, nutritious food, and adequate space.

Dozens of color variations exist among zebra finches. This species is dimorphic, so there are visible physical differences between the sexes. The male has cheek patches, usually orange, barring on the throat, and a bright colored beak. The female is duller in color, does not have cheek patches, and no barring on the throat. See Figure 3-9 to see a true pair. Sex is a little more difficult to distinguish in the pure white mutation. In the white zebras, the male has a brighter red beak and the female beak is more orange.

FIGURE 3-9: A male and a female zebra finch.

WARNING

Zebras can be slightly aggressive at breeding time and occasionally have dominance issues in a larger group, especially if they're crowded. Make sure your zebra finches have enough space and separate any aggressive birds until breeding season is over.

Chapter **4**

Finding and Selecting Finches

inding your perfect pair (or more!) of finches may seem easy at first glance. Just go to a pet store, right? There's nothing wrong with doing that, but knowing your choices *before* you see those particular birds you just can't live without is always a good idea. Almost any pet store that carries birds will have finches, but they may carry only the most common species, and perhaps you're looking for something a little more exotic.

Then again, you may have fallen in love with the first two finches you saw and brought them home on the spot. It happens to the best of us. A sweet little face and a pretty song will steal your heart. Whatever the case, this chapter helps you choose your first finch — or your 50th. Remember, a lone finch will become despondent and stressed. Always keep finches in pairs, except for the canary, which does like to be alone.

Choosing Finches: Exploring Your Options

More than a thousand species of finches exist, though most of them are not available in the pet trade. Among these many different species are an absolutely marvelous number of *mutations* (including different color variations) to choose from. Different species have different personalities, too. Chapter 3 provides a long list of finches you may be able to find in your area.

The age of your new finches

TIP

You should look for young adult or newly weaned finches, especially if you're buying zebra or society finches (species that have been kept in captivity for a long time). Remember, most zebra finches live between four and nine years, so if you want to keep your finches for a while, you'll want youngsters.

TIP

How can you tell how old a finch is? Generally speaking, baby finches wear a different color plumage than the adults, sometimes drastically different. Gouldian babies are a drab olive-green color, a far cry from their colorful parents. Baby Java finches are dark gray with a charcoal-colored beak, not the stunning gray with white cheeks and pink beak of their parents. Baby zebra finch chicks look like little gray sparrows, drab brown with a dark beak. (See Figure 4-1.) You would never imagine that these birds will turn into beautiful zebra finches.

FIGURE 4-1:
This baby zebra finch looks nothing like its beautiful parents, but it will come into adult feather within a few months.

kurashova / 123 RF

Because finches mature so quickly, they're in adult feather by 3 to 6 months of age. At this point, knowing how old they are is difficult. Some breeders put a leg band on their babies when they're about 10 days old, and this band may have the year printed on it.

Gender

Do you want a male and a female? If so, you may end up with babies, which seems like a fun thought until you're overrun with babies and you encounter issues that come with breeding finches, such as egg binding, lameness, and so on. (Chapter 9 gives you the lowdown on breeding finches.)

WARNING

Some finch species can be kept peaceably in a single-gender pair or an entire flock of one gender; however, don't keep both genders in the same area in separate cages. This will cause all the birds a lot of stress and can even cause aggression.

Most people keep finches in a male/female pair, so that's probably what you should look for when you're starting out. There are ways to keep your finches from breeding that you'll learn in Chapter 9.

Previously homed finches

Statistically, many birds only stay in the average home for just two years. People give birds up for all kinds of reasons, but whatever the reason, many birds find themselves homeless and cast aside.

TIP

Consider giving a home to a recycled finch. Just because the finch is an adult doesn't mean that you won't experience all the joys of living with these little creatures. Contact your local shelter or breeder and let them know you'd be willing to provide a home for any unwanted finches. You may also be able to find someone giving away finches on an online classifieds site.

TIP

BREEDING FINCHES

To breed your birds, you need to know how to choose good breeding stock. You can't know for sure which finches will make good breeders, so just try to choose the healthiest birds you can find.

Typically, female finches should not be bred at all until they're at least 9 months old, although some species are capable of breeding as young as 3 months (especially the males of the species). If finches are bred too early, the offspring can be weak and sickly.

If you're looking into a cage of finches to choose a pair, look for two birds who are hanging out together and preening, or sleeping on a perch cuddled up together. This may be a pair of birds who have already chosen each other and are already in love.

A few other things can improve your chances for successful breeding. Look for birds that are large for their particular species. Look for clear markings and birds that stand upright and look around alertly. Avoid birds that look too thin or have drooping wings. Also, if you can buy from a breeder who has proven breeding stock and regularly shows finches, you're off to a good start. You'll find more information about breeding finches in Chapter 9.

Finding a Finch

After you've made your checklist for your perfect pair of finches, you have to go out and find them. Fortunately, you can look in a variety of places, and if one place doesn't have what you're looking for, you can try another.

Pet shops and bird shops

Most pet shops carry only the most popular varieties of finches, but first-time finch guardians will probably want to choose one of the popular species, anyway.

Here are some things to pay attention to when you walk into a pet shop for the first time:

>> **When you walk in the door, pay attention to what your nose tells you.** If the store is dirty or smells funky, leave right away.

>> **Look at the water in the birds' cage(s).** If the water is clean, that's a good sign, but if it looks like it came out of a muddy pond, that's a major problem. Leave a store where the water isn't clean, but do the birds a favor and tell the manager on the way out.

>> **Check for food in the birds' cage(s).** If the birds are out of food or if something is wrong with the food, leave. See the manager on your way out and ask that the birds be offered fresh food.

>> **Look for too many birds in a cage.** Birds need room to move, and having too many birds in one cage is stressful for all the birds and can create an aggressive environment.

>> **Look for birds that are inactive, look kind of puffy, are sleeping or standing on the floor of the cage, have puffy or swollen eyes, or have any dried or wet matter stuck to the feathers surrounding the vent.** These symptoms are indications of illness. Leave those birds alone.

>> **Look for generally crowded conditions.** If all the bird cages are tightly stacked and crammed together, you can bet that if one bird has an illness, the others are likely to get it, too.

>> **Talk to the staff and see how helpful and knowledge-able they are.** Can they answer the questions you have or do they just shrug and say they don't know? Also, if the salespeople at your pet shop aren't friendly and helpful, they won't be friendly and helpful when you get home and have a problem, either.

A birds-only shop is a better option if you have one in your area. The staff is likely to be more knowledgeable about birds and you will find more variety both in the species of finches and in the items that they need to be healthy and happy.

Whether you purchase finches or canaries from a general pet shop or a birds-only pet shop, be sure to ask some questions about your potential finches before you consider taking them home. Here's a good place to start:

>> **Where do you get your finches?** If the answer is, "Some guy drops them off," or "I don't know," reconsider buying from that store. If the answer is, "We get them from a breeder who takes great care of the birds," that's a better answer. If the salesperson says, "The owner breeds and hand-raises them herself," that's the best answer you can get.

>> **Do these finches come with a health guarantee?** If the salesperson says, "What's that?" run fast and far away from the place. The store should be willing to take back the bird within a certain number of days if it doesn't get a clean bill of health from your avian veterinarian.

>> **What are these finches eating?** "I dunno," is a terrible answer. "Seeds, what else would they eat?" is equally poor. If the answer is that all the birds are fed seeds or pellets plus fruits and vegetables and other fresh foods, you're likely to be happier with a bird from that store.

>> **How old are these finches?** The store employees should be certain of the birds' ages.

Swap meets and flea markets

You can often find finches sold at your local swap meet or flea market, but be aware that if you buy a pair of finches from a swap meet, you may not be able to find the person who sold them to you the next week. Try to get a business card or a phone number when you purchase your birds.

The classifieds

Sometimes breeders advertise in online classified ads and on finch forums. The breeder may be a small-time home breeder with a few pairs and some babies to sell. This breeder may be a good choice because you may get to see where your bird came from and may even make a friend in the seller, a person who can help you if you have trouble with your finches.

Be careful about going to people's houses when you pick up your bird. Talk to the person on the phone a few times and take someone with you. Never go alone. Listen for birds in the background on a phone call. If you don't hear any, be careful. Don't let the person come to your home either. Meeting in a safe, neutral place for the exchange is always a good idea. Odds are you won't have a problem, but remember that this is a stranger. Online dating rules apply!

Breeders and experts

If you're very lucky, you'll find an actual finch breeder, someone who breeds for color mutations and for showing. This person can even become a mentor to you, helping you become more knowledgeable in the hobby if you choose to breed your birds.

When you arrive at the breeder's home, look for cleanliness and check to see if the birds are being treated humanely. Do they have enough space? Do they have fresh, clean water? Is the temperature too warm or too cold? If you feel comfortable with the conditions of the birds, then you should be comfortable buying finches or canaries from this person.

Ask for a health guarantee and the right to return your finches if they don't get a clean bill of health from your avian veterinarian.

Bird shows

If you're extremely lucky, you may find a bird show in your area. Very often, avian breeders from around the country bring their birds to show and sell. A bird show is a great place to meet people and to see all kinds of different species and colors of finches.

Walk around the show and talk to everyone. Take some numbers and make some friends. These people know the most about your finches. They can help and advise you with any situation you may encounter. Maybe someday you'll be the finch expert and will be able to help someone new to the hobby.

Searching for a Healthy Finch

When you've decided on the color, age, and type of finches you want, you now have to go about choosing a healthy pair, which is actually easier than you think. Check out the following sections for tips on what to look for in healthy finches.

Eyes

A finch's eyes should be bright and shiny. No crust or discharge should be coming from the eyes. The eyes should not be puffy or swollen. A finch's eyes should show an attitude of alertness, as the Gouldian finch's eyes do in Figure 4-2.

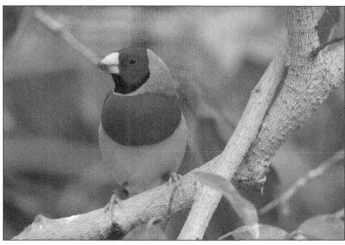

FIGURE 4-2:
Your finches' eyes should be alert, bright, and free from debris.

etfoto / 123 RF

Nose and nares

A finch's nostrils are called *nares*, and they're located at the top of the beak where it meets the bird's face. The nares should be clean and without discharge.

Listen to the finch's breathing. If you hear a clicking noise, this could be indicative of air-sac mites. Check for an overgrown beak, which is also an indication of a health problem.

Feathers

The feathers of a healthy finch are bright and shiny, lying flat against the body. A finch with excessively ruffled feathers may be ill, but this isn't always the case. Feathers can get ruffled if the bird is being picked on or if he has recently traveled in a small space with other finches.

Feathers should cover the whole body. If you notice bald patches, the finch has a problem. He may just have a feisty cagemate plucking a few of his feathers, but you can't be sure. Avoid finches with any bald patches.

Feet

A finch should have two feet (preferably), with four toes each (three forward and one back). The feet should be free of debris and any scaly patches, which may be a sign of mites. The finch should be able to perch easily on both feet. However, if a finch's wings are intact and the bird only has one foot or is missing toes, it will be able to navigate the world just fine.

Vent

The *vent* is at the bottom of the bird and is the place where waste is eliminated and where eggs are laid. The vent should be clean and dry, not wet or crusted with feces or other material. You should also check for prolapse, which could be an indication that the bird has produced many eggs and is undoubtedly older than advertised.

TECHNICAL STUFF

A *prolapse* is when part of a bird's intestines or reproductive organs fall out of the *cloaca* (where eggs and feces come out). You'll easily be able to spot this if the finch you're looking at has it.

Attitude

Healthy finches are cheerful, alert, and busy, busy, busy, always on the move, interacting with cagemates, eating, flying, grooming one another, cuddling, quarreling, and mating. Their energy is incredible. If the bird you're looking at seems lethargic or tired, this could be an indication of trouble, or it could just be nap time. Either way, before you commit to buying that particular bird, check back later to see if its energy level has increased.

HEALTH GUARANTEES

As with anything else, *buyer beware.* If you buy a finch without a health guarantee and it keels over, you're stuck with a dead finch and no recourse. Most good stores and breeders allow you a certain amount of time to take your bird for a checkup and will take the bird back if your avian vet finds a problem. If you buy a bird without a health guarantee, you're buying the bird at your own risk.

You may be tempted to buy the sleepy, sick looking bird. Of course, if you're a bird lover, how can you turn away from it? Do what feels right to you, but buying a sick bird is often a mistake. You risk infecting your other birds, you'll incur a sizable veterinary bill, and the bird may not survive anyway. You're better off starting out with healthy birds that will cause you the least worries.

Housing Finches Together

Try not to house a finch alone for long. Most finches like to be in pairs, though some finches, such as canaries, are territorial and won't want to be housed with other finches when it's not breeding season.

That said, don't crowd your finches either. If you want to house more than one pair, increase your cage size accordingly. Also, if you're planning to mix species of finches, talk with an experienced breeder to determine which species can live together and which species interfere with each other when breeding. Each pair of finches should have in excess of two square feet of space to themselves. If you're going to mix species, this is best done in a large aviary or habitat setting with many nesting sites and visual obstacles, such as bushes and trees.

Some pairings known to work — and not work — include the following:

>> Society finches do well with zebra finches, parrot finches, cordon-bleus, cherry finches, whydah finches, strawberry finches, and Gouldian finches.

>> Gouldian finches can be housed with zebra finches if your aviary is large enough, though zebras can be pushy and may interfere with the Gouldian finches' breeding.

>> Zebra and society finches can be housed with non-aggressive parrot species such as budgies, Bourke's parakeets, and cockatiels, but there must be enough room in the aviary for all of them to get out of the way of each other and to nest when and where they choose.

>> Weaver finches should not be housed with any other type of finches.

>> Java finches can be housed with other peaceable finches, but the aviary must be very large. (See Figure 4-3.)

>> Canaries can only be housed together when they're breeding. Otherwise, they should be kept in separate cages.

FIGURE 4-3: This Java finch and zebra finch can be housed peaceably together if given enough space and resources.

ijphotostocks / 123 RF

Caring for Your Finches

IN THIS PART . . .

Preparing to bring your finches home

Feeding your finches properly

Grooming your finches

Getting to know your finches

Chapter **5**

Home Tweet Home: Preparing for Your Finches and Bringing Them Home

When you've found your perfect pair (or more!) of finches, or perhaps an adorable canary, you're going to need to get ready to bring the birds to their new home, and that involves a lot more than just putting them in a cage and leaving them some food and water. This chapter shows you some of the ways to house your finches and how to accessorize your finches' home so that they stay happy and healthy.

Your Finches' New Home

Very few finches are *finger-tame*, which means that giving them opportunities to fly free in your home requires effort, preparation, and time, and those opportunities may not come all that often. You may not always have an extra couple of hours to spend catching your wandering finches. Chances are that your finches will spend the majority of their time in their cage or aviary. No cage can ever replace flying free, but the more spacious you can make it for them, the better.

WARNING

Finches need to fly for exercise, and if their cage is too small for them to fly, their health will eventually suffer.

Size matters: Cages, flight cages, aviaries, and habitats

At an absolute minimum, a cage for a single pair of finches should measure 36 inches in length by 24 inches in width by 18 inches in height — but that is strictly a minimum. Instead, look for the absolute largest cage that the space in your home and your budget will allow. The horizontal dimensions (the dimensions across) are more important than the height. *Remember:* Your birds *must* fly to stay healthy.

Long, rectangular cages are better than round cages for finches. Finches won't take advantage of the height of the cage as much as they will the back-and-forth flying space.

WARNING

Regardless of the size of the cage, the spacing of the bars or mesh still matters. Most popular finches are tiny creatures, and they can be seriously hurt or killed by getting stuck or hung between the bars of a cage. The spacing should never be greater than ¼ inch between the bars.

A *flight cage* is typically a free-standing, very large cage that offers your birds a lot more room to fly and is a good choice if you want to breed your finches. A flight cage isn't usually large enough for a human to step into, but it's large enough to allow your finches to feel a little bit of freedom.

When you're ready for your feathered family to grow, you may want to consider an aviary. An *aviary* is a large cage designed to hold several pairs of finches, even dozens. An aviary can be situated inside your home or outside, and it should be large enough for a human being to enter. An aviary affords your birds a far greater opportunity to fly than a standard cage does, and it allows your finches to follow their natural group-living instinct. An aviary also lets you make your finches' home a lot more interesting. You can add more types of perches and some nontoxic, natural tree branches. If you're planning to do any serious breeding, you'll certainly need an aviary, but even if you're not, considering one is a good idea.

Habitats are generally much larger than aviaries, and they mimic the species' natural environment as much as possible. In addition to plants, habitats usually include running water. Habitats are nearly always located outside, giving your finches an opportunity to enjoy the fresh air and sunshine.

Take care when you house your birds outdoors to protect them from predators and weather. Non-tropical finches can live outdoors year-round, but they must be acclimated to the weather by being outside when the seasons change. If you keep them inside where it's warm and then put them outside in the extreme cold, the temperature change can be shocking for them and they may die. Finches can even handle snow and ice, but they have to be the species of finches that come from climates where winters are similar to yours.

A good rule is that your finches should be housed in the same basic temperature as they would have in their native wild habitat.

Considering cage materials

Metal and plastic cages are suitable for finches, as long as they're constructed with nontoxic materials and contain no zinc (no "galvanized" metal). See Figure 5-1. Be wary of the coatings used to cover metal cages. If it starts to flake and your birds ingest it, they can become extremely ill and even die.

FIGURE 5-1:
The mesh
that makes
up this cage
is the
correct size
for these
male zebra
finches.

chiyacat / 123 RF

If price is no object, you may want to look into some of the wood and acrylic cages available these days. Some of them are exquisite pieces of furniture and help to eliminate a lot of mess. Of course, their prices reflect that. I've even seen DIY projects online where people turn gorgeous display cabinets into finch flight cages.

WARNING

Wooden pagoda-type cages are unacceptable for finches. Although they're very popular and look great, they tend to harbor moisture, bacteria, and fungus, and they can become home to parasites that may affect your birds' health. Stick with materials that are easier to clean.

Keeping cage safety in mind

WARNING

Finches are surprisingly hardy, but they can be fragile, too. Fancy or elaborate metalwork on a cage can catch a tiny toe and break it or tear the nail. Scrollwork and round cages with bars that taper together as they reach the top pose a choking hazard if a bird gets their head caught.

The cage bottom should have some kind of mesh or grating about ½ inch or more above the liner. This is to keep the birds from walking around in their own mess. The best liner for the bottom of the cage is plain old newspaper. The ink has disinfectant properties, and you can easily see how much mess needs to be cleaned up. However, since newspaper is becoming obsolete (and you don't want to line the cage with your tablet!), you can purchase blank newsprint sheets or rolls quite inexpensively. This white paper also helps you to see your birds' waste more easily, which helps you see if there are any changes, such as blood or undigested seeds in the droppings.

WARNING

You may be tempted to use bird litter, but I don't recommend it. When you use litter, seeing if one of your birds has a problem (by looking at the droppings) or if the cage needs cleaning is made more difficult, and the litter also holds moisture, which allows bacteria and fungus to grow.

If you have a walk-in aviary or habitat, a good bottom is a simple concrete slab that you can hose down daily. Some people also use clean sand at the bottom of the aviary, rake it daily, and change it completely a couple of times a year. Sand is a good substrate if you also want to keep small quail with your finches. You can use cheap play sand from any hardware store, the kind that goes into a kid's sandbox.

Deciding where to put your bird's cage

TIP

Your finches will be happiest with their primary residence against a solid wall or in a corner. If you can't find a location like this, cover one side of the cage with something solid, like a dark cloth. Finches feel insecure and frightened if they're out in the open and can't get away because they're trapped in a cage.

REMEMBER

Finches are a prey bird, always on the lookout for the approach of a predator. With a solid surface or two to make them feel protected, they'll relax and settle in far more readily.

Place the cage in an area that will see a bit of activity, but not too much activity. Your finches are stimulated by watching things happen in the room, but they'll be uneasy if they're in the middle of chaos.

Small, tropical finches are susceptible to cold. Place the cage well away from any drafts. Ideally, the room where they live should remain at a constant temperature. Choose a spot that gets a lot of ambient light during the day, preferably natural light. The location should also be a quiet place during the night hours. A small amount of direct sunlight is very good for your birds' health, but they should be able to escape from it if they want. Direct sunlight can get much too hot for them very quickly.

WARNING

There are some places where you should *never* place your finches' cage. These include the following:

>> **The floor:** A high spot will make your finches feel safe. A low spot will make them uneasy, especially if you have other companion animals or small kids.

>> **The hallway:** Hallways have too much foot traffic.

>> **A child's bedroom:** Small children should only interact with finches under close supervision. These tiny birds are too easily injured to survive being handled by a small child. Even if your child is older and responsible, a child's room will be uninhabited for much of the day, which doesn't give your finches much to see or hear unless you keep the television or radio on for them.

>> **The bathroom:** The temperature and humidity fluctuate too much here.

>> **The kitchen:** Kitchens have lots of temperature changes, and the fumes emitted by nonstick cookware are deadly to birds. (Avoid nonstick cookware even if your birds are in another area of the house. Fumes can easily travel through doors, walls, and ventilation systems.)

>> **Directly in front of a window:** Your birds will be frightened by neighborhood cats and anything else unfriendly that passes by. The headlights of cars may frighten them, as will the sun bouncing off cars' windshields. Even more important, too much direct sunlight can make the cage far too warm.

QUARANTINE: WHEN, WHERE, WHY, AND HOW

TIP

When one of your birds is ill or when you introduce a new bird to your home or aviary, you should establish a quarantine procedure. In the case of new birds, this is a matter of putting them into a different room, far from your other birds, for a period of 40 days. You don't want to risk exposing your other birds to a potentially fatal illness. Some people quarantine for 30 days with good results. If you do notice something wrong with your finches, seek veterinary care for them immediately.

Separate a sick bird from your other birds as well. Place it in a hospital cage by itself, in a location where it won't be disturbed. To create a hospital cage, use a 10-gallon aquarium or similarly sized plastic container made for small animals. Provide a mild heat source — a heating pad or lamp placed under or on one-half of the cage that brings the temperature inside the cage to about 90° F (32° C). Make sure that the bird is able to move away from the heat source if it becomes too warm. Check the cage several times to be sure that your bird isn't too warm. If the bird is too sick to get around the cage well, place food and water on the floor of the cage, where the bird can get to it easily, and make sure the water dish is very shallow, or risk the bird drowning. A quarter inch of water should be fine.

Maintain the finch's normal daylight/nighttime schedule, if possible. If you normally cover your birds at night, you should cover the ill one, too, but make sure that covering your heating source will not make the housing too warm.

Accessorizing Your Finches' Abode

Finches need a few specific accessories to keep them happy and healthy. However, make sure not to clutter a cage so much that your birds cannot fly back and forth. With that in mind, here are some things that your finches need.

Perches to stand on

Your cage probably came with a couple of perches, and they're fine, but variety is important. Your birds spend a lot of time on their feet, so they need a variety of materials, widths, and textures to stand on to keep their feet healthy.

WARNING

Be sure not to position perches above food and water dishes, and leave plenty of room in the cage for unobstructed flight. If you crowd the cage, your finches may injure themselves flying into the perches in a panic.

Wooden perches

Not all wooden perches are plain pine dowels. See Figure 5-2. Manzanita perches come in some unusual shapes, and cholla wood is nicely textured. You may even want to use a branch cut from one of your own trees, with the bark still on it, as long as you're sure that the wood is nontoxic and has never been sprayed with insecticide or fungicide. The rough coating of bark is good for your finches' feet, and it will also help to keep their claws worn down. Most hardwoods are safe, as are pine and fruit trees, such as citrus, plum, pear, and apple. See Figure 5-3.

FIGURE 5-2: Your finches will enjoy natural wooden perches of varying sizes.

nancyb / 123 RF

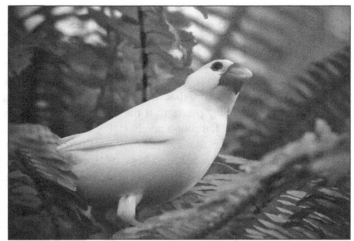

FIGURE 5-3: This white Java finch is enjoying its time among natural, nontoxic ferns.

The drawback to wooden perches is that they require frequent cleaning. Wood absorbs biological materials that decompose and can grow colonies of bacteria. Wooden perches need to be scrubbed thoroughly at least once a week. About every ten days (or at least twice a month), soak them in a 10 percent solution of chlorine bleach and water (9 cups water to 1 cup bleach). Be sure the perches are thoroughly rinsed and completely dry before returning the perches to the cage.

Plastic perches

Plastic perches, like the ones that probably came with your cage, are very easy to clean and snap on and off at various places around your cage. However, they're probably not as comfortable for your finches as natural wood.

Rope perches

Rope perches have traditionally been used for parrots, but several brands of tightly twisted cotton rope perches are made especially for finches. You want tightly twisted rope perches so that they won't snag your finches' tiny claws. If you notice the rope fraying, remove the perch and toss it. You don't want to come home to a finch who has hung itself on a loose thread or gotten a foot caught and broken a leg as a result.

Concrete and rough perches

Finches will appreciate concrete and rough perches. You'll find many available, of all shapes and sizes. I recommend offering three sizes of rough perch: skinny, made perfectly for finch feet; medium, to ensure that their feet get a stretch; and quite large, so that when they perch on it their feet are flat or almost flat (you can also find flat rough perches). Because birds like these perches so much, offer them as the top-most perch in the cage, because your birds may want to roost on it. Also, keeping rough perches at the top will help them not to become soiled as frequently.

Cups and bowls

TIP

Plastic is not a great choice for your food and water dishes. It scratches easily and retains bacteria in the crevices. Instead, opt for ceramic or stainless steel. Stainless steel is outstanding because it's easy to clean, hygienic, and absolutely safe for your birds. Both ceramic and stainless steel dishes are available with the hardware to snap in and out of the cage. If you notice that the ceramic is becoming *crazed* (filled with small, hairline cracks), replace it to avoid bacteria growing in the crevices.

TIP

If your finches throw seeds out of the cage so frequently that walks through your living room sound like you're striding across the sand at the beach, you should consider a seed dish with a hood. Your finches can then fling away without dumping the entire cup of seeds.

Buy two (or more) complete sets of dishes for your birds, and you'll have a much easier time keeping them clean. Soak one set in a 10 percent bleach solution once a week (or more) while the other is in use and make sure to rinse thoroughly before using them again.

TIP

A special type of cup is made to hold one-half of a boiled egg, an outstanding treat for your finches. Feeding finches a lot of egg when they're breeding is important, so this cup is especially useful at those times.

Some people like tube-style waterers for finches because the water can sometimes stay cleaner longer in the tube and there is less area for the birds to toss food and droppings into it. However, just because the water lasts longer doesn't mean you don't have to change it every day. I recommend against these tube-style waterers: Simply use a shallow dish (or more than one) for water.

WARNING

You will also need a third cup for soft, wet, and fresh foods. Don't ever put wet or moist food in the seed or pellet dish, as these dry items can mold and grow bacteria when wet.

Cage covers

Most birds feel more secure having their cage covered at night, and finches are no exception. A cover provides darkness and protects finches from nighttime movement in the house, perhaps a cat slinking about in the night, or mice scuttling around. The cover also protects finches from drafts, and the darkness inside the cage may allow you to sleep a little longer if your birds like rising with the sun.

REMEMBER

Make sure that the cage doesn't become too warm with the cover in place. Also, be sure that your finches don't develop *night frights,* a kind of birdy panic attack that generally happens when they hear or see things at night that frighten them. If they do panic at night and thrash around the cage, possibly injuring themselves, cover only three of the four sides of the cage so that the birds have a bit of light and use a nightlight if the room they're in is too dark.

Mineral blocks and cuttlebones

A cuttlebone is an absolute necessity for your finches. It's the internal skeleton from a type of squid or cuttlefish, and provides a great source of calcium. A mineral block is also a good source of calcium and helps your finches keep their beaks trimmed.

Toys

Typical finches and canaries are not as interested in toys as parrots are, but because they spend most of their lives in a cage, giving them some interesting things to do is a good idea.

TIP

With finches, the key is to keep it simple. Small ladders and swings, preening toys, a small bell (not a jingle bell style, which can catch toes), and a mirror should do the trick.

MITES AND MOTHS AND BIRDS, OH MY!

A *mite protector* is a small can that hangs on your birds' cage and contains an insecticide. It isn't very healthy for your birds, and it isn't absolutely necessary either. Although your birds can pick up mites, if you keep the cage clean, visit your veterinarian often, and observe a quarantine period for any new birds introduced into your household, they're unlikely to develop a serious problem. If you do suspect that your birds have mites, call your avian veterinarian and ask whether you can use Sevin dust or diatomaceous earth as a remedy. Both of these powders kill mites, but your birds should not come in contact with it.

The *seed moth* is a type of moth that sometimes arrives in bulk seed. It won't harm your birds, but if you find that you have a problem in a batch of bulk seed, put the seed in the freezer. Protect your other dry goods by putting them in plastic bags or containers, and then purchase a trap that attracts the moths using their own *pheromones,* which are kind of like hormones that the other insects can smell.

Be careful with mirrors. You'll enjoy watching your finches interact with that "other" bird, but if your birds start to feel that their territory is being violated, they can become stressed. If your finches attack the mirror, remove it from the cage. Canaries in particular can change their behavior for the worse if there's a mirror in or near the cage.

Baths

Your finches need to bathe. Bathing keeps their feathers and skin in good condition, and it improves their sense of well-being. Most finches bathe several times a week, sometimes every day, even when breeding. The eggs need moisture to remain healthy (yes, eggs need to be healthy!), so the female will bathe and bring moisture back to the nest on her feathers.

Before deciding on a bathing setup, remember that birds drown very easily. They don't need to immerse themselves to get a bath — in fact, giving them a bathing arrangement that's too deep is dangerous. A flat, shallow dish with about ½ inch of water in it is perfect for finches. See Figure 5-4. Your finches will wade in it, splash in it, flutter their wings, and scatter droplets in it. Your finches will also cheerfully drink their bathwater despite having a separate water dish, so change their bathwater daily.

TIP

Once in a while, and only if they seem to enjoy it, you can spray your finches gently with a fine mist from a spray bottle. If they like this gentle misting, they'll let you know by lifting a wing and turning this way and that to get the spray right where they want it.

FIGURE 5-4:
Finches love bathing, like this red-billed firefinch.

aoosthuizen / 123 RF

Lighting

If you live in a cold part of the country, or if you aren't able to provide your finches with direct sunlight, you can purchase a bird lamp with a broad-spectrum light bulb, one that's made specially for birds or reptiles. Or you can put the bulb in an ordinary cheap spotlight that you purchase at any hardware store. These lights do a pretty good job of imitating sunlight. They aren't perfect, but they're better than nothing.

Your birds need this broad-spectrum light to synthesize vitamins and remain healthy. If your birds are breeding, they'll need either sunlight or full-spectrum light about 14 hours per day. You can also take your finches or canary outside on a sunny day in a smaller cage and sit with them to enjoy the sunshine. Always supervise and don't do this if the birds are breeding and have eggs or chicks.

Heating

If you live in a cold climate or you like to keep your air conditioner at arctic temperatures (like I do!), your finches will appreciate a heat source. You can use a spotlight with a full-spectrum bulb, as mentioned above, but that won't keep your finches warm at night. I recommend investing in two different items. First, a heated perch. This should be the top-most perch in the cage, as your birds will likely want to roost there at night. Second, a snuggle up heater. This item looks like a flat rectangle that you attach to the bars of the cage near a perch. It emits a low-level heat (kind of like a heating pad) and your finches can snuggle up to it when they feel cold.

Keeping Mess Away

Even if you have only one pair of finches, the mess in your home may multiply. These busy little darlings find some truly inventive ways to scatter mess. You can get the situation under control without resorting to demolition or a daily housekeeper.

Cage bloomers and seed guards

Cage bloomers and seed guards both fit around the bottom of the cage and help to keep the scattered seeds and vegetables in the cage tray.

TIP

If your birds are truly talented at seed flinging, bloomers and guards may not be enough. One method that seems to work is to purchase some clear plastic from a fabric shop or online and cover the back and sides of the cage with it, leaving the top and front open to the air. You may even need to put a small flap of plastic in front where the food and water dishes sit.

You can also purchase some inexpensive clear acrylic sheets and affix them to the sides of the cage where you hang the cups. You don't need to cover the entire side of the cage for this to be effective.

Cleaning supplies

One of the most important investments you can make is a small hand vacuum. If you leave one of these little hand vacuums a few feet from your finches' cage, contending with mess is a lot easier. An automatic robot vacuum is also handy, especially one that you can program to run around the floor a couple of times a day.

Most things you're accustomed to using to clean up stubborn messes are toxic to your feathered friends. Instead, try the all-natural route: Baking soda makes an excellent scrubber, and vinegar is an outstanding disinfectant. But don't use them together — the chemical reaction is quite startling!

If you're lacking in the spirit of cleaning adventure, you can find several safe-for-birds commercially prepared cleansers that do a fair job and smell pretty good. But you'll still need to do some scrubbing.

Change the paper in the bottom of the cage daily or at least every other day. Scrape dried droppings once a week from the floor grate, perches, and anywhere else you see dried waste. About every ten days, soak the entire cage in soapy water and disinfect in a 10-percent chlorine bleach solution. Rinse and dry thoroughly before returning your feathered friends to their home. If your cage is large, you'll ideally have a hose nearby and a high-pressure nozzle (just make sure that you don't power-wash any of your birds!). You can certainly clean more often, but this is a good start.

HEPA filters

Birds create bird dust from their feathers and their droppings can dry and aerosolize, so if you keep your finches or canaries indoors, you may want to invest in a HEPA filter. Just make sure that it doesn't have an ozone ionizer option (typically used for odors), or that you can turn it off. Ozone isn't safe for birdy lungs. Fortunately, your cage, your birds, and their droppings do not have a bad odor as long as the cage is clean enough.

Setting up the Cage

There are a few details to keep in mind when you're setting up the cage. First, don't overcrowd it. Your birds should be able to fly without running into things. Secondly, never place perches over food and water dishes. Finally, place one or more perches at the very top of the cage, as this is the perch where your birds will probably roost (sleep) at night.

Many cages have doors for the food and water dishes at the bottom of the cage. Although many finches are ground feeders, having the food and water dishes too low can result in a lot of droppings in them. Instead, toss those little plastic dishes and place stainless steel or ceramic dishes higher in the cage, ideally near a perch.

Finch-Proofing Your Home

If you plan to allow your finches free-flight time, even if you think that you're going to supervise them all the time, you have to finch-proof your home. Even if you have a pair that's *never* going to leave the cage, the average home has things that can be harmful, even deadly, to finches and canaries.

TIP

Here are a few tips to keep your birds safe:

>> **Make sure all windows are screened.** Finches are excellent fliers.

>> **Remove frilly, lacy curtains.** A finch can hang a tiny claw in them and become trapped and injured. If you don't see it happen, the bird could go into a full-blown panic attack and die.

>> **Keep your windows and mirrors a little dirty.** Yep, you heard me right. Windows and mirrors should be covered, be a little dirty, or have stickers on them, because your finches may mistake the glass for open space and fly into it.

>> **Get rid of the ceiling fan.** Your finches may fly up there while it's on. Enough said.

>> **Eliminate all substances that produce fumes or scents from your home.** Finches have an extremely delicate respiratory system. Fumes that may not bother you, like those from a scented candle or an air freshener, can kill a finch. When it's heated, nonstick cookware also emits fumes that are proven to kill birds. (See the list later in this section for information on which common household products include this coating and should be avoided at all costs.)

>> **Put all medications out of reach of your finches.** Those pills may look like tempting treats for your finch and the result could be deadly.

>> **Make sure your finch can't access standing water.** Water such as that in a fish tank, fountain, or dog water dish poses a drowning threat to a finch. A finch can even drown in a glass of water while trying to take a drink.

>> **Remove all toxic houseplants from your finches' reach.** Quite a large number of common houseplants are dangerous for your finches. These include — but are definitely not limited to — bird of paradise, daffodil, hyacinth, mistletoe, and all types of ivy. A complete list of toxic plants would need a volume of its own, so if you have questions about any plants, ask your veterinarian or do an online search.

>> **Keep predators away.** Although you may not think of them as predators, your companion cat, dog, ferret, rat, and snake can be deadly for your finches. Your cat is always thinking of ways to get close to your finch because they look like tasty snacks and fun playthings, and many dogs have a strong prey drive as well. If you keep your finches outside, they can become prey to raccoons, opossums, hawks, and other predators. Make sure that all outdoor cages are double-wired to prevent other animals from getting inside.

>> **Keep temperature changes to a minimum.** Your finches come from a wide variety of climates and can adapt to a reasonably wide range of temperatures if they're in good health. In any case, avoid rapid changes in temperature and drafts. If your finches are overheated, mist them with cool water and position a fan so it's blowing near them, but

not on them. If they're too chilled, immediately warm them up in a hospital cage (see the sidebar "Quarantine: When, where, why, and how," earlier in this chapter, for tips on creating a hospital cage using an aquarium).

>> **Never allow your finches free flight when you're cooking.** More than one finch has met its demise in a pot of boiling water or cooking oil.

>> **Use a bedspread with a very tight weave.** Bedclothes are a good place for your free-flying finches to get tangled up and hurt.

>> **If your furniture has any loose-weave upholstery, cover it.** Your finches may get hung in the weave and injured.

WARNING

Products that use nonstick coating (and that should be avoided at all costs) include the following:

>> Anything that says it is "nonstick"

>> Bread machines

>> Broiler pans

>> Coffeemakers

>> Nonstick cooking utensils

>> Crock pots

>> Curling irons

>> Deep fryers

>> Drip pans for burners

>> Electric skillets

>> Griddles

>> Hair dryers (with nonstick coating inside)

>> Heat lamps

>> Ironing-board covers

>> Irons

>> Lollipop molds

>> Pizza pans

>> Popcorn poppers

>> Portable heaters

>> Roasters

>> Rolling pins (the nonstick variety)

>> Stockpots

>> Stovetop burners

>> Waffle makers

>> Woks

Traveling Safely from Store to Home

If you buy your finches at a pet store, they'll send you home with your finches in a temporary carrier that resembles a cardboard box with breathing hole in it. You may as well purchase a travel carrier at the same time that you purchase your finches. You'll need to transport your birds to and from the veterinarian, and you may need a safe place for them while you're thoroughly cleaning their cage or taking them somewhere.

A small cage can work well while you're doing a cleaning, but it's not great for travel. Instead, purchase a plastic or soft-sided carrier with mesh, holes, or bars that are appropriately sized for finches. A carrier with an opening in the top rather than on the side is preferable, because it makes it easier for you to catch the finches without much risk of them flying out.

TIP

If your birds will be in the travel carrier for a long time during a car ride, supply a small dish of seed and some oranges cut in half. You can offer them water for a few minutes every couple of hours, but don't leave water in the travel cage while you're driving. It could spill and make your birds miserable until they dry off again.

WARNING

Don't use perches inside the travel cage. Finches can fly into the perches and get injured. Also, perches may injure finches if the birds are being jostled around in a moving car. Your finches will be fine on the bottom of the carrier.

When you're driving, make sure that the travel cage isn't sitting in direct sunlight, as finches can be overcome by heat very quickly. If the weather is chilly, bring a towel and cover the carrier with it. Never leave the birds in the car in extreme temperatures, below 50° F (10° C) or above 90° F (32° C). If the temperature is warm, be sure the bird has water at all times.

TIP

Finally, buckle in your birdy friends. A seatbelt should have no problem going around the carrier, and you can even put it through the handle on top.

Chapter **6**

Caring for Your Finches

Y ou've brought your finches home and you've prepared a nice home for them. Now what? In addition to the many hours of pleasure you can expect in watching your feathered companions, you're also going to have some responsibilities. Finches are complex and active creatures, and they have some definite needs. No, you won't have to spend 24 hours a day caring for them, but you need to do some things correctly if you want your companions to be happy and healthy.

Water: Extremely Essential

Like all living creatures, finches need an ample supply of clean drinking water. In the wild, the search for water takes up a great deal of a finch's time and energy.

Besides providing plenty of water, keep in mind the following suggestions:

>> **Place a variety of water dishes in different locations in the cage at all times to minimize competition and quibbling among birds.** A bully finch may not let a meeker finch drink, and this can be deadly.

>> **Place at least one water dish in the lower part of the cage so that a bird who may be feeling a little under the weather doesn't have to fly to a perch to drink.** Finches can become dehydrated to a life-threatening degree in a matter of just a few hours, so if you're busy or preoccupied for a relatively short period and fail to notice that one of your birds isn't getting to the water dish, this can be fatal.

>> **Use either bottled drinking water or filtered tap water — but never water straight from the tap.** The additives in tap water are not good for your finches (or for you, for that matter). Filtered tap water is the cheapest solution over time, but make sure that the filter is a good one. The best option is bottled drinking water. *Remember:* Your finches won't make a distinction between their bathing and drinking water, so their bathing water should come from a filtered source also, and it should be as clean as their drinking water.

>> **Change all water in your finches' cage or aviary at least once daily.** Two or three times per day is even better, especially if you pass the cage and it looks like your birds have had a mud bath in their water dishes. This is affectionately called "poop soup."

TIP

Making water changes is easiest if you have multiple sets of water dishes and rotate them morning and evening or more often, if necessary. Soak the dishes in a 10-percent bleach solution once a week and rinse thoroughly before replacing them in your finches' cage.

REMEMBER

If you use a tube waterer (which I don't recommend), change water daily to keep your companions' water clean and free of bacteria and filth. It doesn't matter what the package says — a two-week waterer still has to be changed daily!

Knowing What Your Finch Should (and Shouldn't) Eat

The most important thing to understand when it comes to feeding your finches is that finches actually have two diets — one for the breeding season and one for the non-breeding season. The differences are minor but extremely important.

Ideally, you want your finches to have a diet as close to their natural diet in the wild as possible. This means offering a wide variety of carbohydrate and protein sources. In the following sections, I fill you in on which foods and supplements are healthy to offer during all seasons.

Seed and pellets are only the beginning. In the wild, your birds would also have access to a variety of vegetation and live insects. Though most finches can survive for a while on seed alone, they are unlikely to thrive or breed well on such a diet. In the following sections, I tell you which foods your finch will favor.

Seeds and pellets

Finches come from all over the world, so what they eat in different locations is somewhat different. Each species likes a slightly different seed mix for this reason. Goldfinches, for example, like a mixture of canary seed, nyjer, rapeseed (canola), and hemp; zebras and society finches prefer a mix of yellow, white, and panicum millets, Japanese millet, spray millet, and small canary seed. Many commercial mixes of finch seed are available.

TIP

All labels show ingredients, and some labels indicate the species the seed is best for. A little checking of labels will show you the mix ideal for your finches.

TIP

If you notice that your finches regularly leave a certain type of seed in their dish and voraciously eat other types, you'll begin to get an idea of what your finches like. Buying seeds that your birds don't eat is a waste of money. Instead, you can make your own mix by buying in bulk the seeds they like and create your own blend.

Don't be taken in by highly priced, specially fortified seeds with vitamins and pretty colors. These mixtures have extra vitamins in the coating on the shell or husk of the seed. Because finches don't eat the husk, the vitamins don't do them any good.

Some people recommend substituting specially formulated pellets for seeds, but pellets are different enough from your finches' natural diet that you may have considerable difficulty convincing your finches that the pellets are for eating. Finches nearly always prefer real seeds, but there is certainly no harm in offering pellets.

Be certain that whatever pellets are offered are formulated for finches, and never, ever make the birds go cold turkey when changing them from seeds to pellets. Instead, mix the seeds and pellets and change the ratio of seeds to pellets gradually so that, eventually, all you're serving is pellets. *Remember:* Finches can die if they don't have food for several hours, so don't starve them.

Because your finches hull their seeds, it will often look like a whole bowl of seeds is waiting to be eaten, when in reality what you're seeing is just hulls, the part of the seed that the bird leaves behind after it eats the inside. Even if you see a "full bowl" of seeds, adding new seeds every day is important. Also, toss the seed dish often to make sure the seeds and hulls aren't moist, which can lead to mold.

Veggies and fruit

Veggies, especially dark green and orange veggies, are wonderful for your finches. These contain vitamin A, an essential nutrient. Fruits in these colors are wonderful as well. The more variety, the better. Try offering fruits and veggies chopped, shredded, cooked, and mashed — you can even clip washed greens to the side of the cage or weave them in between the bars. Make sure to wash everything very well before you feed it.

Birds are individuals, just like people, and their likes and dislikes vary widely. Some things your birds may love include grated Brussels sprouts, grated carrots, shredded romaine lettuce, kale, spinach, cucumber slices, melon, broccoli heads, alfalfa sprouts, whole-wheat bread, and cornbread.

Here's a list of vegetables that are good for your finches:

- Beet tops
- Beets (raw or cooked)
- Bell pepper
- Broccoli
- Brussels sprouts
- Carrots (raw or cooked)
- Celery
- Chard
- Collard greens
- Corn
- Dandelion
- Asparagus

- Endive
- Green beans
- Green pepper
- Jalapenos
- Kale
- Mustard greens
- Pumpkin
- Spinach
- Watercress peas
- Yams (cooked)
- Yellow squash
- Zucchini

Never leave fresh foods in your birds' cage for very long. Two hours to about half a day should do, depending on the weather. If you live in a warm climate (or if it's summertime), make sure that fresh foods don't spoil.

An extremely easy thing to do is to buy a bag of frozen mixed vegetables at the supermarket and thaw small amounts daily for your birds. Frozen veggies aren't as good as fresh ones, but they're great when you're busy. Chop them into fine pieces so that they're easier for your finches to eat.

Most finches love fruits. Fruits are excellent sources for some of the vitamins your little companions need. Some things to try include apple slices, banana, pear, honeydew, cantaloupe, grapes (with skin), peaches, plums, and figs. If you like it, your birds probably will, too.

Make sure that fruit is always fresh. Don't leave fruit in your birds' cage overnight.

Here's a list of fruits that are good for your finch:

TIP

- Apples
- Apricots
- Bananas
- Berries (any variety)
- Cantaloupe
- Cherries
- Figs
- Grapefruit
- Grapes
- Honeydew melon
- Kiwi
- Mango
- Oranges
- Papaya
- Peaches
- Pears
- Pineapple
- Plums
- Watermelon

Snacks

You can have a good deal of fun with your birds when it comes to snacks. Preparing healthful treats for your finches is fun. When those treats are good for them, watching them go wild over something new and particularly tasty is even *more* fun.

TIP

Finches love hard-boiled egg. Egg is an important source of protein and vitamins for them, especially when they're breeding. Mash up a bit of very-well-cooked hard-boiled egg and put it in one of their dishes. I guarantee a show! Include the shells — they're a great source of calcium. When you make eggs, rinse the eggshells thoroughly, microwave them for 4 minutes or bake them at 350° F (175° C) for 45 minutes to kill salmonella, which is as deadly for your birds as it is for you. Then dry them, crush them, and offer them in a separate dish. Eggs with the shell provide an important source of calcium.

TIP

Commercially prepared *egg food* is also a nutritious treat for your finches and is critical for finches that are nesting and feeding chicks. It's also great for weaning baby finches and for molting, sick, and stressed birds. It is typically made from dried eggs, honey, flour, and a variety of other ingredients. You can also easily make your own. A quick online search will yield dozens of recipes.

FINCH TREAT STICK RECIPE

You can purchase commercially prepared seed sticks, but it's more fun and nutritious to make your own. Here's how:

1. Find a safe stick, such as wooden chopsticks, unsalted pretzel rods, and Popsicle sticks.

2. Mix a cup of bird seed, a cup of finch sized pellets, a cup of oats, a half cup of chopped dried fruits, a half cup of millet flour or brown rice flour, a quarter cup of honey, and two egg whites. Add a tablespoon of calcium powder or a crushed-up cuttlebone to the mix.

3. Wet the ingredients slowly by pouring in small amounts of apple juice until the mixture is moist enough to form into balls. Make sure it's not too moist, or it won't hold together. If you've added too much juice, add more oats until it's dry enough.

4. Pack the mixture around the stick you have chosen using your hands.

5. Place on a cookie sheet and bake at 200 degrees for 40 to 60 minutes.

Store in the refrigerator and serve one stick every other day or so.

Millet spray is another fun treat. Though seeds are part of your finches' staple diet, the process of figuring out how to get them out of a millet spray tied to the side of the cage affords lots of enjoyment for both you and your birds.

Live insects

Your finches need protein. In the wild, they obtain much of their protein from live insects, and they should ideally receive live insects from you, especially when they're breeding. The easiest way to provide this is with commercially purchased insects. You can breed them yourself, but few people want to go through this trouble, though it's a fun project for school kids. Mealworms are very easy to raise, and you get the benefit of being able to feed them to your finches when they're very small and soft.

Your choices include mini-mealworms, waxworms, white worms, fruit flies, maggots, and fruit-fly larvae. When your finches are not breeding, offer them live insects two to three times per week if you can. During the breeding season, your finches will want some live insects daily.

Table foods

If you exercise a little common sense, your birds will enjoy and benefit from almost anything that you can eat. With the exception of a few things (which I outline later in this chapter), they can have some of just about everything on your plate.

Obviously, you should avoid feeding them some foods, but the ones you should avoid are not good for you either. Avoid excessive salt and foods that are very fatty or greasy, the sorts of things that your doctor tells you to avoid. Soft whole-wheat bread is great, as are crumbled wheat crackers, as long as they aren't salted.

TIP

Offer pound cake in tiny amounts to your finches on a semiregular basis to get them used to eating it. Yes, you should avoid offering them processed foods and sugars almost all the time, but pound cake is a great way to get your finches to take medicines when they need them. You can coat or soak the pound cake in the medication and then feed it to the birds.

Cooked foods

Several companies now offer cooked foods for various species of birds, including finches. Generally, these are excellent, easy, and convenient diets for birds.

TIP

Most cooked foods for birds expand when cooked, some as much as 100 percent. Check the labels carefully so you don't prepare too much. You can refrigerate cooked food for a few days, but it will go bad soon after that.

You can also make your own cooked foods for your finches, such as cornbread, for example, adding pellets, peas, dried fruit, seeds, and most anything else they like. You can make whole-wheat pasta and melt soy cheese over it and then sprinkle pellets on top if you want to get really inventive. Just don't serve it too hot.

Fun Finch Food Recipes

Here are three easy recipes that your finches will love.

Finch flapjacks

Purchase whole-wheat or buckwheat pancake mix. Make the batter as directed on the box, and then add dried fruit, veggies, well-cooked egg (including shells), finch pellets, and anything healthful you have in the house (remember that wet ingredients will make the pancake mix too moist). Cook well and cool before offering. Freeze and offer part of one thawed pancake a day along with other foods. Making the pancakes tiny will make them easier to serve. You can also make this recipe into waffles.

Finch fiber fusion

Grains are great for finches. If you want to get inventive, you can make up a batch of grain food every week and have a nutritious, warm meal for your feathered pals each day.

Using the directions on the boxes, make a serving each of quinoa, amaranth, brown rice, whole oats, and whole-wheat couscous. Cook them separately and then mix them all together. You can also add whole-wheat pasta as well if you like.

Next, soak and cook a few types of beans, such as lentils, red beans, black beans, garbanzo beans, and so on. Or, if you're in a hurry, open a few cans of beans, rinse them, and then add them to the grain mixture. For a really nutritious treat, sprout the dry beans before you cook them.

Finally, fold in shredded carrots, yams, chopped jalapeno peppers, peas, broccoli, kale, frozen soybeans, frozen peas, and anything else you have in the house that's healthy and safe to feed your finches. Add a sprinkle of cinnamon and calcium powder. Freeze in ice cube trays. Heat on a plate in the microwave to slightly above room temperature and offer one serving a day.

Finch fries

You can make healthy "finch fries" in an air fryer, toaster oven, or your regular oven (if any of these have nonstick coating, be sure that your finches aren't in the area when you're cooking). Slice some root vegetables, such as sweet potatoes, beets, and carrots into sticks about the size of a French fry — you can also use hard squashes and zucchini. Place on a baking sheet and slow roast at 300° F until tender. Serve slightly warm. Keep the remainder in the refrigerator and serve daily.

What not to feed your finch

WARNING

Here is a list of the things you must keep your little hungry companions away from:

>> **Chocolate:** Chocolate is toxic for birds.

>> **Avocado:** This tasty plant harbors an ingredient near the skin of its pit that is toxic to birds.

>> **Onions:** Onions aren't good for finches.

>> **Alcohol:** Never allow your finch to sip an alcoholic beverage.

>> **Pits and fruit seeds:** Some pits and fruit seeds are dangerous. Don't take the chance. Remove them from fruits before offering to your finches.

>> **Mushrooms:** Not good for finches.

>> **Spinach and chard:** These are fine foods for your finches when it's not breeding season. Though they have many nutritious vitamins in them, they also have oxalic acid in them that binds calcium, making it unusable in the body, and when finches are in breeding season, they need the calcium.

>> **Salt:** Salt is toxic for finches.

>> **Caffeine:** Caffeine is not good for birds and can be toxic.

The best general rule is to avoid junk foods. Keep your finch well away from the foods your doctor tells you to avoid yourself.

Nutritional supplements: When food is not enough

REMEMBER

All finches should have a cuttlebone available, tied to the side of their cage, because it provides a constant and reliable source of calcium and keeps their beaks in good shape.

You may choose to provide your finches with additional vitamin supplements, although if your birds eat a sufficiently varied and nutritious diet, supplements shouldn't be necessary.

WARNING

In some cases, too high a dosage of vitamins can be as bad for your bird as a deficiency. Always follow the instructions for dosage on any supplement you administer to your birds. When in doubt, ask your avian veterinarian.

WARNING

The most common type of vitamin and mineral supplements for finches is a liquid supplement to add to their water. Liquid vitamin supplements can cause your finches' water dishes to become a breeding ground for some dangerous types of bacteria. Change water dosed with supplements more frequently. In addition, don't sprinkle liquid supplements over seeds, because this will cause the seeds to become rancid very quickly.

Don't put powdered supplements directly on seed. Your birds hull their seeds, and in the course of doing this, all the powder will end up in the bottom of the seed dish rather than inside your birds. Instead, sprinkle powdered supplements on mini-mealworms or veggies and fruits.

TECHNICAL STUFF

A heated controversy exists within the bird community on whether or not to offer your finches any type of grit. They probably won't need grit to digest their foods. On the other hand, ground oyster shell and crushed (and sterilized) eggshells are important sources of calcium for your finches. With other forms of grit, such as crushed charcoal or sand, the finch may overeat and the grit could become impacted inside your feathered friend's gut, which can be life threatening. If you talk to five different finch experts, you'll get five different opinions on whether you should offer grit to your finches and how much you should offer. The safest solution is to discuss this at length with your avian veterinarian or other finch hobbyists in your area.

Helping Your Finches Get the Exercise They Need

Finches fly all day long inside their cages, which is the reason that large cages are so essential for these birds. If the cage is large, particularly the horizontal dimension, and contains room for flight between perches without anything in the way, your birds don't ever need to leave their cage.

WARNING

You may want to allow your finches to enjoy free flight from time to time as a treat. If you do this, be certain that the environment is safe for your finches. Watch for loose-weave upholstery items, frilly curtains, standing water, and other things that could harm your birds.

TIP

You'll also need to explore safe ways of catching your finches to return them to their cage or aviary. Many pet shops sell a variety of nets for this purpose. Bird nets have very fine mesh. However, most finches will readily return to the cage when you offer a treat inside, such as millet spray, and most will go back into the cage at night to roost, especially if you've provided a nest.

Getting a Good Night's Sleep: Putting Your Finch to Bed

The key to a good night's sleep is darkness and natural silence (in other words, the regular noises of night, not the television or ringing phone). Most people cover their finches' cage at night, which usually keeps them quiet and safe. It also protects them from drafts and helps to keep anything from disturbing your birds.

Some finches don't like being covered and may become frightened and agitated by unseen movement in the room. If that happens, cover only a portion of the cage, so that your finches still have a good view of the room, and use a dim nightlight near the cage.

TIP

One advantage with a good cage cover is that your finches' cage will remain dark for a longer period in the early morning and may prevent your finches from waking with the sun and tweeting you and your family right out of bed.

Grooming Your Finch

Grooming your finch isn't like grooming a dog or even a parrot. You don't have a lot to do with the grooming process — you can pretty much leave it to the finches unless there's an issue.

WARNING

WING CLIPPING: A DEFINITE NO-NO

A common practice with many larger companion birds is to clip the primary flight feathers to make flying more difficult for the bird. This is often necessary during taming, and many people choose to clip the bird's flight feathers throughout the bird's life.

Do not clip your finches' flight feathers! Finches fly for their exercise. They don't climb like parrots, and they're rarely finger-tamed. Their one and only true exercise is flight. If you prevent your finches from flying, their health and well-being will suffer.

The only time anyone ever clips a finch's wing feathers is if a particularly aggressive male is in an aviary during breeding season. The bird keeper may choose to gently clip two of the flight feathers on each wing just to slow the bully down a bit — but not to prevent them from flying. Don't do this yourself. Ask an expert or your avian veterinarian.

Toenail clipping

Any bird's toenails can become unpleasantly sharp and over-grown and may require clipping. Sharp nails can get caught in rope or nesting material and can harm eggs in the nest. You can minimize overgrown nails by maintaining several perches in your finches' cage that are rough in surface texture, like concrete or sand-covered perches.

The first hurdle to clipping your finch's toenails is catching the bird. An easy way is to note the finch's location in the cage and turn off the lights, then reach inside and grasp it gently. In a larger aviary, you'll probably need to purchase a finch net (which is made of very fine mesh) to catch your birds.

TIP

No matter how you catch your finch, you need to make sure you hold the bird correctly for toenail clipping. Your hand should sur-round the finch, snugly but without squeezing. Be certain that you don't cover your finch's *nares* (nostrils). Hold the finch in your left hand (or right hand, if you're left-handed), and secure the foot between your thumb and index finger, so that the foot doesn't wiggle during the procedure. Your finch will try to curl their feet close to their body. Your finger grip should be firm enough to prevent this without injuring your finch. This can be easier with two people.

WARNING

A finch's toenails are very small. Just like in other animals, a blood vessel extends nearly to the tip of the nail. This blood sup-ply is called the *quick* (see Figure 6-1). Because of your finch's tiny size, a small mishap that would produce little more than a drop of blood from your cat or dog can be life-threatening to your finch. Be sure to clip in a very well lighted place. If your finch has light-colored nails, you'll be able to see the quick of the nail (the blood supply). Do not cut into the quick! If the nails are dark, cut only the very tip. Be conservative.

REMEMBER

Keep a supply of veterinary styptic powder (not the kind used on humans) on hand to stop bleeding if you do have a mishap with your bird. Don't try to apply the powder to the nail. Instead, gen-tly insert the nail into a dish or container of the powder and wait for the bleeding to stop. If you wait for bleeding to stop naturally without using styptic powder, your bird may become weak or even die. A bar of soap works in an emergency, as does baking flour.

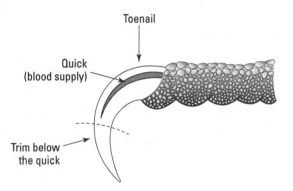

FIGURE 6-1: Do not to cut into the quick when you trim your bird's nails.

For a clipping tool, human nail clippers will work very well, if you use care in clipping. Clippers for human baby nails are great. Round nail clippers used to clip cat nails are good as well.

TIP

If you're in any doubt as to how to clip your finch's nails correctly, take it to the avian veterinarian. Your vet should be able to do a good and safe job of clipping your bird's toenails in the office and may show you how to do it safely at home as well.

WARNING

NEVER GROOM YOUR FINCH'S BEAK

Trimming a finch's beak is a very delicate procedure. Because a mistake could easily prevent your bird from eating, you need to be sure that beak-trimming is done by a veterinary professional (if it's necessary).

Problems with a finch's beak can occur from injury, mites, genetic problems, and malnutrition. This can result in an overgrown beak, a misaligned beak, or a crusty beak. A veterinarian should address any beak issues.

A cuttlebone helps to prevent beak issues. A finch, like any bird, will clean his beak on a rough perch or cuttlebone immediately after eating, which helps keep the beak from overgrowing. A cuttlebone has the added advantage of providing additional calcium in your bird's diet.

Bathing your bird

Finches love to bathe. Moisture is necessary for the health of your bird's feathers and skin. Provide a clean, shallow dish of room-temperature water (use filtered or bottled water, free of chlorine, and not more than ½- to ¾-inch deep), and change the water frequently. Your finches will dip their beaks in the water and drink from it. They'll also splash about and flap their wings a lot, scattering water droplets. This is another good reason for situating your finches' cage over a floor that can be cleaned easily!

TIP

Make a clean bath available for your finches daily. Finches will bathe several times a week at least, and most will bathe every day. Remove and replace soiled water promptly.

TIP

In the rare event that you have a finch who seems suspicious of a bath, or who is reluctant to bathe for another reason, you can use a mister to spray the bird by hand. The spray should be very, very fine and gentle and always applied from above and behind your bird. Some birds love being sprayed with a mister and will raise their wings and turn this way and that under the light spray.

WARNING

Be careful not to drench the cage or nest. Never spray your finch in the face.

Giving your molting birds some TLC

Molting refers to the process of feathers dropping off your bird and new ones growing in to replace them. Although loss of feathers at the wrong times can be a sign of stress or illness, molting is a perfectly normal process for any bird and does not indicate poor health.

When you see feathers at the bottom of the cage, it's probably the result of normal molting. Take your bird to the vet if you see feathers at the bottom of the cage and if any of the following is true:

>> Your finch stops eating.

>> Your finch spends more than half the day sleeping.

>> You see bald patches on the bird.

Molting usually happens when there are changes in light, such as the days growing longer in the springtime and shorter in the winter. Captive finches often molt several times in a single year.

Even though molting is completely natural, it does cause an unusual amount of stress for your bird, and it needs some additional care during these periods. When your finches begin to molt, they'll sleep more than usual. After a day or two, you'll begin to notice fallen feathers at the bottom of the cage. A few days into the molt, your finch will probably look a little scruffy and threadbare. This is normal. As the new feathers begin to grow in, the bird will spend an unusual amount of time preening, and you may think the bird is repeatedly scratching an itch, when it's actually just helping the pin feather (new feather) sheaths to break. Resist the temptation to treat for mites unless you're certain that your finches have a mite issue.

Additional calcium, protein, and egg food help a great deal during the molting process. In addition, give your birds plenty of access to direct sunlight. Sunlight helps their bodies produce vitamins and hormones that help with the molting process. *Remember:* Make sure that they have a shaded area to retreat to — direct sunlight can become too warm for your finches very quickly. Let your birds decide how much or how little they need.

Your birds can breed during molt, but it isn't a great idea. If possible, prevent breeding by not providing nesting material for them. Both breeding and molting are very stressful periods for your birds — so why combine the two if you can avoid it?

As the molt continues, you'll notice *pin feathers* appearing all over your bird, giving the bird a spiky appearance. New feathers, called *pin feathers,* are covered in a hard, tight, keratin sheath so that they can break through the skin. The finches preen to pull these sheaths off the new feather growth. The sheaths will disintegrate into a fine dust on the bottom of your bird's cage and sometimes the floor surrounding it. This is also normal. Bathing will help the sheaths to become soft and easy to preen away. Your birds know what to do.

Molting periods vary widely among species. Sometimes the bird doesn't come out of molt at all. This situation is referred to as being *stuck in the molt,* and it's usually due to dietary or health problems. Consult your avian veterinarian in the event that this happens to any of your finches. You want to correct this situation as quickly as possible. If your finch is losing feathers and not growing new ones, their cagemates may harass them, and they may even lose the ability to fly.

Can't We All Just Get Along? Living with Other Pets

Finches are delicate, sensitive animals, and they won't "get along" with other companion animals. More likely, your other animals will want to eat or kill your finches. Dogs, cats, snakes, ferrets, rats, and other similar animals all pose a threat to your finches. Keep other companion animals away from your birds.

WARNING

Although your goldfish won't leap from its bowl or tank and kill your bird, the fish tank or bowl can pose a drowning threat to a finch that's allowed free flight in your home. A deep dog or cat water bowl can be dangerous as well.

Some finches can get along with some other species of birds if they are all given enough space, as in a very large aviary. For example, zebra finches, society finches, and Gouldian finches can all live together with cockatiels and budgies (parakeets). Even though these species *can* live together, you must always watch for squabbles and separate aggressive birds. Larger parrots will not get along with finches.

Cleaning Your Finches' Housing

You must keep your finches' housing clean in order to keep them healthy. Clean the paper or litter beneath the bottom cage grate at least once every other day, daily if you can. The grate will also become soiled, so clean it at least once a week, twice a week if you have time.

Perches will become soiled with feces and food, so remove them when they look dirty and wash them in soapy water, being sure to rinse well and dry them before replacing them. Once a month (or more), soak perches in a 10 percent bleach solution (9 parts water to 1 part bleach), and rinse and dry well before replacing. Do the same for food and water dishes.

WARNING

Do not, under any circumstances, use *any* household cleaners to clean any part of your finches' cage, dishes, or toys. The best cleanser is warm, soapy water and a clean, freshwater rinse.

TIP

A vinegar-and-water solution in a spray bottle makes a great disinfectant (one-part white vinegar to one-part water). You can also add some fresh lemon juice to make it smell nice. You can spray it on the cage, perches, and toys, and then scrub using baking soda, but be sure to rinse everything well.

Grapefruit seed extract is a wonderful, natural disinfectant and can be found in most health food stores or online. Fill up a spray bottle with water and add one drop of extract per ounce of water. You can spray it on everything your finches touch because it's nontoxic and can't hurt them. Don't spray it on the birds at this concentration, however, because it's bitter and can irritate their eyes and nostrils. Rinse everything well with water after disinfecting.

Grapefruit seed extract is also great for keeping drinking water clean, and it's safe for your finches to drink in small quantities. Adding one drop per eight ounces of water should help keep bacteria at bay, especially in warmer weather.

Remember, when your finches are breeding and they have eggs and chicks, this is not the time to do a big, dismantling cleaning of the cage. Do the best you can to clean without disturbing the birds too much.

Chapter **7**

Come Here Often? Getting to Know Your Finches

Unlike parrots, finches generally don't become attached to people; they just go about their business as they would in the wild, and because of this they are absolutely charming to watch. This chapter helps you recognize normal and abnormal finch behavior and gives you some tips on how to hand-tame a finch.

Understanding Finch Behavior

If you've never lived with companion birds before, much of their behavior probably seems incomprehensible. Take heart: Your finches are not that difficult to understand. With a few simple pointers, you'll know your birds' needs with ease.

What did you say?: Normal finch vocalization

Finches are very social creatures, and social interaction within the flock requires a certain amount of noise. Zebra finches and most of the other Australian exotic finches have a fixed number of vocalizations broken into two categories, calls and songs:

>> *Calls* are short vocalizations meant for communications. A contact call, for example, keeps immediate neighbors in a flock together. Another louder call serves to maintain contact between mates that are some distance from one another, or to keep an entire flock together. A different call signifies warning or aggression. Your finch's calls might just sound like "meep meep" or "wheet wheet" to you, but they actually mean something to other finches.

>> *Songs* are longer and more complex than calls. The male sings to attract a mate, to keep her, and to get her into breeding condition. Females are biologically programmed to want to mate when they hear the male's song. The male also uses song to keep other males out of his territory. By singing, he lets them know he's there. Females rarely sing, though some individuals will sing a bit, but generally not the complex songs of the male.

By watching your birds, you'll come to understand what their vocalizations mean. For example, if you hear your male finch make a certain vocalization when he wants his mate to return to the nest, and he does this every time he wants her to return, you'll be able to recognize that vocalization when you're out of the room and you'll know what your finches are doing. When the male is singing, you'll know that he's likely in breeding condition and he's trying to get the female ready as well.

Fortunately, finches aren't loud, but they are persistently noisy. Most of the sounds your finches will make will be soft chirps and tweeps, inoffensive to all but the most noise-sensitive among us. Finches, like most birds, don't make noise at night, so don't worry about getting a good night's sleep.

You scratch my back, I'll scratch yours: Preening and allopreening

Your finches probably spend a lot of time grooming, and you may wonder if they're just obsessed with their looks. There's a real reason for what your birds are doing. This self-grooming is called *preening*, and it helps them to maintain the preen gland oil in their feathers, which helps to keep them waterproof, and also helps to keep them clean.

If you have two finches paired off, they'll groom one another. This is called *allopreening.* One partner will sidle up to the other and turn to expose the part of its body that it would like to have groomed; the other party will gently oblige. It's very sweet to watch.

Stretching: Birdy yoga

Finches stretch just like humans do and for the same reasons. They extend a wing, a leg, and sometimes both at the same time on the same side, which is called *mantling.* Males also stretch their necks when they sing.

Hungry anyone? Finch vomiting and regurgitation

Just like humans, birds can vomit, which is a distressing behavior that is usually the result of illness, overheating, or poisoning. If a bird is vomiting, you'll notice it shaking its head to remove the vomit from its beak. You may see dried and crusted vomit around its beak and/or on his chest.

WARNING

If you notice your bird vomiting, get it to the avian veterinarian right away.

However, if the bird is showing no other sign of illness, it's probably simply *regurgitating* — which means that it is bringing up partially-digested food from his crop (food that has never reached his gizzard and never been digested) to feed hatchlings or to feed a hen as a part of courting her or so that she can feed the nestlings. This behavior is a sign of affection, part of the breeding process, and completely normal.

Resting on one leg

A finch rests on one leg to conserve body warmth. The behavior is usually accompanied by somewhat fluffed-up feathers. It's part of the normal sleeping posture and only healthy birds show this behavior. Worry about a bird that's regularly sleeping on two feet. Don't worry; the arrangements of muscle and tendon in a bird's leg won't allow it to tumble off the perch.

Scratching

Finches scratch during molting, when the bird is replacing old feathers with new ones, and it's an itchy time for a finch's skin. Finches also scratch when they have a regular itch, just like humans do.

Scratching is sometimes an indication of feather mites in finches. If you notice your finches scratching a lot, and they aren't molting, take your finches to a veterinarian to get a diagnosis and then treat the condition if the doctor suspects mites.

Sleeping and roosting behavior

Finches like to sleep all night, just like you do. They aren't active at night because any activity, especially noise, will alert nighttime predators to their location. A healthy finch sleeps on one leg, possibly with its head turned around and resting on its back (See Figure 7-1). Many finches have nests to sleep inside, so they'll sleep snuggled comfortably on the nesting material.

Finches go to roost every night just after dusk (or in a home where lights are on at night, they'll go to roost when the lights are turned off). (See Figure 7-2.) This means that they find a safe, snug, comfortable place to sleep where they feel protected from predators. If your finches have a nest or hut of some kind, they will roost for the night there. Some finch species will cram into a nest in numbers that you wouldn't think possible!

If you don't provide your finches with a nest, they will want to roost as high as they can in their cage, so make sure that you provide some good perches high up in their housing. When you see where they prefer to sleep, hang some fake plants around the area to make them feel extra safe.

TIP

Should you cover your finches at night? If their area is drafty in the evening or gets cool, you'll want to cover three sides of the cage. It's not a good idea to cover the entire cage because they do need some air flow. You might also want to keep a nightlight in the room where they sleep so that they aren't startled by things going bump in the night. (See Figure 7-2.)

FIGURE 7-2:
This
Gouldian
finch is
sleeping
with his
head
tucked onto
his back, a
completely
normal
sleeping
behavior.

Romeo, oh Romeo: When your finch goes a-courting

Courting behavior differs among species of finches. Some fire-finches and waxbills will present the female with a long blade of grass, indicating a desire to build a nest. Others, including the zebra finch, sing to a prospective mate as well as bend down in front of her and brush his bill back and forth. See Chapter 9 for more information on breeding behavior and breeding your finches.

Finch Communication

Finches in the wild communicate using calls, songs, and body language. Finches in captivity do the same. Some finches are very social, like zebra and society finches, and they'll all want to eat, bathe, and nap at approximately the same time.

Communicating with your finch will probably be pretty basic. You can talk softly and soothingly to your finches, sing to them, make clicking noises, and whistle. You may or may not get a response from them. Each finch is different, and whether they respond to you has everything to do with how much human contact they had when they were young and how much they trust you. Because finches are kept in pairs or groups, they'll be busy communicating with each other and won't have a lot of reason to communicate with you, and that's fine. Just let them be themselves.

Handling Your Finch Safely

There are very few reasons to handle your finches. You may need to clip long nails at times, or you may need to move birds from one cage to another, or take them to the veterinarian, but these are pretty much the only reasons to handle your finches. If you have a tame finch, that's another story — but most people don't.

If you simply want to move finches from one cage to another, you can use a net specifically made for birds. This net has a very fine mesh that the bird's nails can't get caught in, unlike a fish net that can easily catch a bird's toe.

If you need to handle your finch for any reason, you can simply grasp the bird very gently with your bare hand. You don't need gloves — your finch won't hurt you. A parrot's bite will hurt, but a finch's bite won't, and it's unlikely that a finch will try to bite anyway. He'll be too scared to do anything but squirm.

Grasp the bird firmly enough to keep it in your hand, but don't squeeze it. Constricting a bird around the chest will prevent it from breathing. Only hold the finch for as long as you require to complete the procedure. Finches can panic and even die if they're extremely frightened.

Taming Your Finch

Unlike parrot-type birds, most people don't tame or train a finch. The best you'll probably get out of a finch is for it to tolerate your presence in the room, or perhaps it will come to trust you enough to hop over to the side of the cage and take a worm from your hand. If you're a very patient person, you can try allowing your finches to fly in a bird-proofed room where their cage is, and you can sit nearby, quietly, holding a treat. Eventually the finches may come to you (see Figure 7-3).

If you breed finches, you may have the opportunity to hand-raise a finch if the parents toss it out of the nest, abandon it, have too many babies to care for, or die. Handfeeding finches isn't easy, but many people do accomplish it. Handfeeding isn't without risks for your finches, so it's a good idea to get hands-on advice and help from a finch expert in your area who has successfully handfed finches before. Don't handfeed finches just to have tame pets — many babies being handfed do not make it to maturity.

cynoclub / 123 RF

FIGURE 7-3:
This Java
finch's
guardian
has
hand-
tamed this
feathered
friend.

3

Training and Breeding Your Finches

Chapter **8**

Keeping Your Finches Healthy and Handling Emergencies

P art of taking care of your feathered friend is making sure that it's healthy and getting help when it's not. In this chapter, I help you find a veterinarian for your birds, figure out when you should go see the vet, and identify the different signs and symptoms of some finch illnesses.

The Veterinarian: Your New BFF (Bird Friend Forever)

For your finches' medical care, you want an *avian veterinarian*, a vet who specializes in the care and treatment of birds. The best place to find an avian vet in your area is by calling the Association of Avian Veterinarians at 720-458-4111 or by visiting www.aav.org.

Regular examinations

Most people don't take finches to a veterinarian for regular check-ups the way you would a dog, cat, or parrot. However, to ensure optimum health and prevent problems before they become serious, you may want to begin a relationship with an avian veterinarian by taking your birds for a general exam when you first get them and ask any pressing questions you may have.

REMEMBER

It's a good idea to take your new finches to an avian veterinarian within three days of buying them. Here's why:

>> If you bought your finches with a health guarantee, you'll have some recourse if tests reveal that your new birds are ill.

>> You'll begin a relationship with the vet, and the vet will get to know your birds and be able to evaluate them better because the doctor will know what your birds are like when they are healthy.

>> Some avian vets won't take an emergency patient unless the bird is a regular client. You don't want to be stuck without someone to call if your finches encounter an emergency.

>> Avian vets often board birds in their offices, though some will only board clients — that way they can be relatively sure that the bird won't bring diseases into their office.

>> You'll get some important recommendations from the doctor, including information on diet and housing.

TIP

Even when your finches are well, you may want to take them to your avian veterinarian at least once a year unless it disturbs their nesting cycle. Your veterinarian will run some routine tests and weigh your birds. This *well-bird check-up* will allow your veterinarian to keep records of your healthy birds and will make it easier to determine when they are ill.

Emergencies

When you have an emergency involving your finches, you *must* take them to an avian veterinarian right away. So what qualifies as an emergency?

TIP

If you have *one single moment* of worry about something that has happened to your bird (it has flown into a window, broken a toe, is bleeding, and so on), or if you notice a drastic change in a finch's behavior, appearance, droppings, or eating habits, you probably have an emergency.

Don't hesitate to rush your bird to the avian veterinarian. Minutes are crucial in an emergency. *Remember:* Your bird is a small, sensitive creature more likely to be overcome by the stress of an accident than a larger animal.

What a Healthy Finch Looks Like

Knowing something about the finch's bodily systems and observing your bird carefully when it is healthy will help you to be able to tell if it's ill.

Eyes

A healthy eye is clear, moist, and free of discharge. A finch with an eye problem may squint or scratch it excessively with a foot, or rub its eye on the perch or sides of its cage. There may also be feather loss around the eye and the eye may appear crusty (see Figure 8-1).

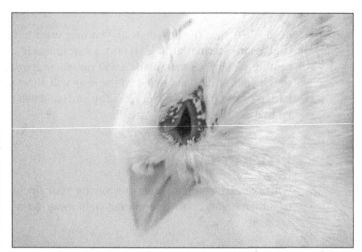

FIGURE 8-1: This canary has an eye issue that needs to be addressed by an avian veterinarian.

TIP

If you see swollen eyelids, cloudy eyes, excessive blinking or discharge, and tearing, have your bird checked out by a vet.

Ears

Your finch's ears are located a short distance parallel from the eyes and look like holes in the head. Each ear opening is covered by feathers. You may get a glimpse of the ear openings after your finches bathe, when the feathers around the head are wet and stuck together.

TIP

If you can see your finch's ear opening without the bird being wet, make an appointment with your avian veterinarian.

Beak

Your finch's beak is made of the same durable material as your fingernails. The beak grows over a basically hollow honeycomb-like structure, a convenient design for an animal that should be light enough to fly. The beak acts as a crushing tool but is delicate enough to peel the skin off a pea.

Your finches should be able to keep their beak trim through eating and playing. If your bird's beak is overgrown, or if the surrounding tissues are crusty or scabby, it could be an indication of a nutritional disorder or mites, and you'll have to take it to an avian veterinarian for treatment. (See Figure 8-2.)

Dr.MYM / Shutterstock.com

FIGURE 8-2: A veterinarian examines this canary that has inflammation around its beak.

WARNING

Never, ever try to trim your finch's beak yourself.

Feet

In addition to walking and grasping, birds also use their feet to regulate their body temperature. When your finches are cold, they may draw one leg up into the body and stand on the other leg. When your finches are warm, the blood flow will increase to their legs, which will help their whole body cool down.

Several injuries are common to the feet, including catching toes on cages and toys, as well as problems with the leg band. Swelling in the legs could be a symptom of *gout* (a painful condition that can be the result of poor nutrition). If the skin on the bottom of the foot is red and inflamed, or even scabby, this could be a sign of *bumblefoot* (an infection associated with poor nutrition and obesity).

TIP

If you notice something wrong with your bird's legs or feet, take it to your avian vet. Contact your avian veterinarian right away if you notice any foot or leg weakness or *lameness* (inability to walk).

Feathers

A healthy finch should be obsessed with taking care of its feathers, preening them for much of the day. A finch likes to keep its feathers neat, clean, and well organized on its body.

Birds *molt* (shed their feathers and grow new ones) once or twice a year, usually during seasonal changes. When your finches molt, you'll notice feathers on the bottom of the cage, but you shouldn't be able to see patches of skin on your birds. If you do notice bald spots, contact your vet — it could indicate a serious medical problem. When a new feather begins growing, it will be encased in a protective sheath called a *pin feather*. Pin feathers can be itchy and your finch may become a little cranky at this time.

Respiratory system

Finches have a very sensitive respiratory system. They react negatively to airborne irritants, such as aerosol sprays, fumes from heated nonstick cookware, and tobacco smoke. They're prone to respiratory illness and distress.

TIP

If you notice your finch panting, call your avian veterinarian and describe the situation. Keep your finch away from fumes and airborne toxins.

WARNING

If you notice a change in your bird's breathing or, in extreme cases, bubbling from the mouth or nostrils, take your finch to the veterinarian right away. Your finch could have a respiratory infection, mites, or possibly poisoning.

Skeletal system

Many of your finch's bones are filled with air, and all of them are thin-walled, which makes them light enough for flight. Though bird bones are strong enough to allow the movement of wings in flight, they're easily broken.

TIP

If you suspect that one of your finch's bones is broken, take it to the veterinarian immediately. Some of the bones contain air sacs that aid in breathing, and your bird may experience respiratory problems if it has broken bones. Symptoms should be relatively obvious — if you see your bird with a leg or wing hanging, or if the bird goes lame, it could indicate a break. Of course, if you see a break (as you would in a human), you'll know right away.

Digestive system

The finch's digestive system begins with the beak and ends with the vent. After your bird swallows food, the food goes to the *crop* near the bird's breast. From the crop, the food goes to the stomach, then on to the *gizzard,* which grinds the food. Then the food moves on to the *cloaca,* where the feces, *urates* (the off-white or yellowish part of the dropping), and urine collect before being eliminated through the *vent.*

Because your finches will probably be munching all day, they will be pooping all day too. This is normal. Frequent elimination is a function of flying — a bird that's holding a load of waste is going to be heavier, so nature gave birds only a small capacity to hold that waste. This means the waste has to be eliminated often.

Waste should have three parts to it — a green solid-ish part, a yellowish white part (urates), and a watery part (urine). Sometimes the color of the waste changes according to what you're feeding your bird. If you feed blueberries or beets, for example, expect the color to change. If you feed greens, expect there to be more urine in the feces — this is normal and isn't considered diarrhea. If you notice a drastic change in your bird's droppings, see your avian veterinarian.

WARNING One common digestive disorder comes from feeding grit to finches. Finches don't need grit the way other types of birds may. If your finch eats too much grit, it can stay in the crop and cause impaction. The crop won't be able to empty and will become distended. You may notice bloody feces with undigested seeds in it.

Signs of Sick Finches

An ill finch will sit quietly in the cage and may sleep a good deal. Sleeping a lot in the daytime is a fairly obvious sign of trouble. In addition, your bird will puff up its feathers, attempting to control its body temperature and stay warm.

There are other signs that may indicate a variety of problems. Respiratory distress (panting), bleeding, a wet and messy vent, or failure to eat, especially if the food offered is of a type your finches have enjoyed previously, can all be signs of illness.

Finches often lose weight rapidly. This is due to a variety of illnesses and should be addressed immediately.

Place a sick finch in a separate hospital cage as quickly as possible to avoid infecting other healthy birds (see "Assembling a First-Aid Kit," later in this chapter). As soon as possible, take the finch to your avian veterinarian.

Any odd behavior may indicate illness, but not always. Finches, like most birds, are creatures of routine, and a sudden break in routine signals that you should investigate your bird's condition.

If you can't find any reason for the unusual behavior, start looking for symptoms of illness, including the following:

>> **Fluffiness:** If you notice that your finch is overly fluffy, it may be trying to retain heat.

>> **Sleepiness:** A sick finch may sleep too much. Sleeping on the bottom of the cage is especially telling.

>> **Loss of appetite:** If you notice that your bird isn't eating, it could indicate a serious problem.

>> **Weight loss:** Weight loss is a sign of a number of illnesses. *Mycobacterium avium* is responsible for the tuberculosis infection and can be transmitted in food, water, or by filthy cage parts. It can be transmitted to humans with compromised immune systems, so be careful to avoid infection.

>> **Change in attitude:** If your finch is not behaving in its usual manner, it may be ill.

>> **Change in feathers:** Lack of grooming and feathers falling out in patches can indicate illness, as can abnormal feather growth. If you notice a change in your bird's feathers, take it to see your avian vet.

>> **Lameness:** If your bird can't use its feet, you can be guaranteed that something is wrong.

>> **Panting or labored breathing:** Either of these symptoms can indicate a respiratory ailment, or perhaps overheating. Changes in your finch's breathing, changes in vocalization, or gasping or wheezing can be a sign of infection. Be sure to take your finch to the avian vet right away if you notice respiratory problems.

>> **Tail bobbing:** If your finch is standing straight up on the perch and its tail is noticeably bobbing, it may have a respiratory problem, or it may just be out of breath from flying.

>> **Listlessness:** A formerly active finch who has become listless and uninterested in life may be ill.

>> **Discharge:** If you notice any runniness or discharge on the eyes, nostrils, or vent, go to the veterinarian immediately.

>> **Food stuck to the feathers around the face:** This indicates poor grooming or vomiting — likely signs of illness.

>> **Sticky substance in mouth or white mouth lesions:** These can be signs of a yeast infection, which can affect the mouth and digestive tract, and can involve the respiratory system. Your finches normally have a certain amount of yeast in their bodies, but when their bodily balance is out of whack, when they are undernourished or after a treatment of antibiotics, the fungus can grow to excess. Regurgitation and digestive problems may occur. Treatment by a veterinarian is necessary. Even though this condition is not immediately serious, it can cause death if left untreated.

>> **Swollen abdomen:** A swollen abdomen could indicate egg binding in a female finch (see Chapter 9 for more information). Consult your veterinarian immediately if you suspect this problem. Normally, an egg is passed within a day of noticeable swelling. Even if she does pass the egg, take her to the veterinarian as soon as you can.

>> **Drastic change in droppings:** Your finch's droppings should consist of a solid green portion, white urates (on top of the green), and a clear liquid. If any of these are discolored (darker green, black, yellow, or red) and there has been *no change in diet,* your bird may have a problem.

>> **Clicking sound when breathing:** This is a symptom of air-sac mites, which is potentially deadly. Mites infest the respiratory system and respiratory distress occurs, followed by death. Products are available to kill these mites, but unfortunately, if your finch is heavily infested, the dead mites may asphyxiate the bird, and you can't do anything to save it. For this reason, many experts recommend treatment for air-sac mites three to four times per year even if no symptoms are present.

>> **Excessive scratching:** This may be a sign of feather mites or lice, which are rarely dangerous, except when the infestation is extremely severe. Even though they're usually not dangerous, they *are* miserable for your finch. See your vet if you notice your finches scratching excessively.

Common Finch Ailments

I mentioned several finch ailments and signs of illness in the preceding section, but you may want to look out for other finch ailments in your flock. Here are a few of the more common culprits.

>> **Aspergillosis:** *Aspergillosis* is a fungal infection caused by fungi spores in the environment. It occurs mainly in birds being kept outdoors, especially in damp or humid environments, or in dry environments with little air flow. It causes fungal pneumonia, which is tough to treat. Birds fed all-seed diets are at risk, as are birds kept in an environment where their lungs are compromised, such as in a home with a smoker. Signs include respiratory distress, weight loss, listlessness, and a change in vocalizations.

>> **Atoxoplasmosis:** *Atoxoplasma* is a parasite that affects the liver and can infect all the tissues in the body. It is particularly an issue for canaries, but other species are prone to it as well. Signs include loose stools and diarrhea, fluffiness and listlessness, and lack of appetite. It usually affects juvenile birds and is around 80 percent fatal.

>> **Avian Polyomavirus:** This virus primarily affects young birds and causes lesions and warts. Signs include lack of

appetite, diarrhea, vomiting, and weight loss. It is mostly fatal, but some birds do recover.

>> **Bumblefoot:** *Bumblefoot* is an infection of the foot that causes red patches and sores on the feet, and if not treated, can cause permanent damage and even loss of the feet. It happens primarily in birds with inadequate or dirty housing and perches and those who are fed an all-seed diet. It is treatable and many birds can heal from it.

>> **Camphylobacter:** The *camphylobacter* bacteria live in the digestive tract and cause digestive illness characterized by yellow droppings that may have undigested seed in it, listlessness, and is often fatal in young birds. Keeping proper avian hygiene is the first step to avoiding this bacterium from flourishing in your flock. This bacterium is also *zoonotic*, meaning that it can be contagious from birds to humans.

>> **Coccidiosis:** *Coccidiosis* is a protozoan infection that attacks primarily the digestive tract. Its signs include blood in the droppings, listlessness, lack of appetite, and diarrhea. Infection spreads in damp environments, especially if the birds' housing is overcrowded. It is treatable.

>> **Cryptosporidium:** This is a gastrointestinal and respiratory protozoan infection that can be transmitted from birds to humans. It is characterized by a long list of signs, including wheezing, lack of appetite, discharge from the nostrils, weight loss, gasping, and listlessness. It is fatal if untreated. Good hygiene can help keep this protozoon at bay.

>> **Scaly face mites:** Signs of scaly face mites include crusty lesions around the face, eyes, beak, and feet. It is treatable and can take up to two months to become fully eradicated.

Emergencies: Knowing When to Get Help Immediately

The average home offers plenty of dangers for finches. Even the most careful of owners may encounter an accident with their birds.

When an accident happens, the first thing to do is contact your avian veterinarian. *Never* underestimate an emergency. If you notice weakness, a fluffed appearance, quick breathing, droopy eyes, the inability to perch, or your bird lying on the floor of the cage, rush your finch to the veterinarian right away.

In the following sections, I cover the more common emergencies. *Remember:* This list doesn't include everything that could happen to your bird, so if you notice something that doesn't seem quite right, don't hesitate to take your bird to the vet.

Poisoning

Poisoning generally happens when a finch gets into a household product. Ingestion or breathing in the poison are the most common ways a finch can become poisoned. Aerosol sprays and other products that leave a fine mist in the air can be particularly harmful for your little bird. Scented candles and plug-in air fresheners may seem harmless, but they can actually cause your finches respiratory distress. Even candle "beads" that are unlit can seem like edible pellets to your finches — and they are deadly when ingested. Items like fertilizers, cleansers, and toxic houseplants are deadly, too. Keep your bird away from *all* household products.

Symptoms of poisoning can include vomiting, paralysis, bleeding from the eyes, nose, mouth, or vent, seizures, and shock.

If you suspect that your finch has been poisoned, try an animal poison control hotline. The ASPCA Animal Poison Control Hotline can be reached 24/7/365 at 888-426-4435. Additionally, the Animal Poison Control Hotline is available 24/7/365 at 855-764-7661. Both charge a consultation fee. Rushing to your avian veterinarian is essential to saving your bird's life, though quick response from you with the help of the Animal Poison Control Center can be crucial.

Animal bites

Animals of all kinds, including your friendly cat, are a danger to finches.

WARNING

When a dog or a cat bites a finch, the wound, no matter how small, can be deadly in a matter of hours, or even minutes. Other animals have bacteria in their mouths that can cause a deadly infection in a bird.

TIP

Even if your other pet was "just playing" with the bird, you should rush to the avian veterinarian right away. In the minutes before you take your bird to the veterinarian, flush a small wound, if you see one, with ⅔ water and ⅓ hydrogen peroxide. If the wound is large, leave it alone and let your veterinarian take care of it.

Overheating

WARNING

If your finch is panting, holding the wings out, standing on two feet, or is even lying on the floor of the cage, it may be overcome with heat.

TIP

Keep a spray bottle handy and lightly mist your finch with cool water, repeating until it's soaked. Watch it closely until its behavior seems normal again. Make sure that it has cool water to drink at all times.

REMEMBER

Finches should never be kept in full sunlight unless they have a cool, shady spot where they can retreat.

If your bird does not respond to misting, remove it from the spot immediately and place it in a cooler environment. If you have a small fan, place the flow of air so that it hits just beside the cage, not directly on it, and mist the bird again. Put drops of cool water in its beak if the bird is unable to drink. Call your avian veterinarian.

Oil on the feathers

Oil on the feathers makes it difficult for a finch to regulate its body temperature, which can be deadly for a bird. The finch may also preen its feathers and ingest this oil, leading to medical problems. How does a finch get oil on its feathers? Believe it or not, finches occasionally fly into a pot of oil (cool oil, you hope!), or may even find themselves in the middle of an oily salad.

If your bird soaks itself in oil and is otherwise uninjured (the oil was cool), dust the bird with cornstarch or flour (any kind except gritty corn flour), making sure to keep the flour away from its face. Remove the excess flour gently with a paper towel. Fill a small, shallow bowl with warm water and add some grease-fighting liquid dish soap. Gently place the bird in the tub and allow it to soak. You may have to repeat this a few times. Do not scrub! Rinse the bird using the same method (without the soap), blot it dry, and place it in a hospital cage with a heating pad underneath half of it and most of the top covered. Don't restrict the flow of air, but keep the heat in. Use a thermometer and make sure the cage is between 80° and 90° F (26° and 32° C). Then take the bird to your avian veterinarian.

Frostbite

Frostbite can cause the loss of toes and feet and may even result in death. If you keep your finches outdoors during the cold season, consider bringing them inside as a preventative on the coldest nights. A finch will hold a frostbitten foot as if it were fractured (frostbite is a painful condition). The frostbitten area will die and turn a dark color.

If you find the condition early, place your bird in a hospital cage with a 90° F (32° C) temperature and call the veterinarian. If you catch the condition at the point where the affected area has already turned dark, get your bird to the avian veterinarian right away.

Unconsciousness

A bird may be unconscious for many reasons, but one strong possibility is that something is poisoning the air. If you find your bird unconscious, ventilate the room thoroughly and remove the bird from the area. Call your avian veterinarian immediately. If you're sure that there is no problem in the air, you can try to rouse your finch by gently handling it and trying to wake it. Get to your avian veterinarian right away.

Egg binding

A swollen abdomen may be a sign of egg binding in a female finch. If a hen is not well nourished, especially if she hasn't gotten enough calcium in her diet, her eggs may have soft shells, which will make the eggs difficult to lay, resulting in egg binding. Egg binding can also occur when the egg is malformed, or when the bird has a tumor or other disorder of the reproductive system. Symptoms of egg binding include panting and lameness. Consult your veterinarian immediately if you suspect this problem.

TIP

Normally, an egg is passed within a day of noticeable swelling. If you notice that your hen is having serious troubles and it's the middle of the night or you can't get to your avian veterinarian right away, move her to a warm (85° F to 90° F, or 29° C to 32° C) and humid hospital cage (see "Assembling a First-Aid Kit" later in this chapter, for tips on making such a cage). Put a few drops of mineral oil or olive oil in her beak with an eyedropper and place a few drops of the same in her vent (where the egg comes out). This may help her to pass the egg.

REMEMBER

Even if she does pass the egg, take her to the veterinarian as soon as you can.

Foot injuries

Don't try to correct a serious foot injury. Place the injured bird in a hospital cage and take it to the vet immediately.

Eye injuries

If your finch's eye has come in contact with an irritant or poison, wash the eye out with saline solution before you take it to the veterinarian. If the injury is from a bite or other type of wound, place the bird in a hospital cage until you can get to the veterinarian.

Seizures

A bird having seizures is in serious condition. Place it in a hospital cage and get to the veterinarian right away. If it comes out of the seizure, you may want to give it a few drops of sugar water or electrolytes to put some sugars into its bloodstream.

Injury to the beak

Often, injuries to the beak can be fixed by a veterinarian, or the beak will heal itself. If your finch has injured its beak, place the bird in a hospital cage and take it to see the vet.

Fractures

Do not try to set a fracture by yourself. If you suspect a fracture, get your finch to the veterinarian right away. A serious break can lead to complications, especially if it occurs in one of the bones containing an air sac.

What to Do if Your Bird Is Lost

REMEMBER

When you first get your finches, take good photos of them to paste on signs and post online in case they ever fly away. Even if you don't have good photos, most finches of the same species look similar, so you can grab a photo off the internet.

Record your bird's vocalizations and keep the recording handy — it may lure the bird down from the treetops when you play the sounds back to it.

TIP

If your bird has already flown the coop, here's what to do:

>> **Watch which way your finch is flying.** Try to keep it in sight as long as you can.

>> **If it has a friend or mate, bring the cage outside and let the two finches talk.** The fly-away may come down to be with its mate. You can put the mate into a small carrier inside a cage with a door twist-tied open. When the fly-away enters, rush to close the door.

>> **Bring all your bird's favorite foods outside and tempt it with them.** Millet spray works well for this.

>> **Bring its cage outside and fill the cage with its favorite foods and lots of water.** It may come down and enter its cage when it gets hungry.

>> **If your finch hasn't come down by nightfall, but you have an idea of where it is, you may be able to climb up and catch him.** A large bird net is helpful for this. Birds don't see well in the dark and are easier to catch at night than they are in daylight.

>> **If you don't catch your bird by the first evening, keep trying the recordings of the vocalizations and tempting it with food**

>> **Make signs for your lost finch.** Place signs within a two-mile radius — finches can fly long distances and you'll want to cover a large area.

>> **Call your local bird club, veterinarians, pet shops, and join local social media lost pet pages and tell them about your lost bird in case someone contacts them about a found bird.**

Because finches aren't tame, your finch probably won't come back on its own. But it is likely that someone will find him, so don't lose hope.

Assembling a First-Aid Kit

The first and most important item in your finch first-aid kit is a well-set-up hospital cage or brooder, with a source of heat and humidity and a way to control them. Any sick, injured, or stressed bird is going to have trouble regulating its body temperature. It needs warmth, a way to slow down dehydration (humidity), and peace and quiet.

TIP

Making a hospital cage is easy. You'll need a 10 gallon aquarium, an aquarium thermometer, a heating pad, a screen top for the aquarium, paper towels, and a towel. Put the heating pad on the medium setting and place it underneath one-half of the aquarium. Place a few layers of paper towels on the bottom of the aquarium. Make sure to put shallow dishes of food and water in the aquarium too — make sure the water is very shallow, because a weak bird can drown in water as deep as 1 inch.

Place the bird in the aquarium; then cover the aquarium with the screen top. Cover the aquarium three-fourths of the way with a dark towel. The bird should be able to move away from the heat if it wants to. Make sure that the temperature in the tank stays at about 98° F to 99° F (about 37° C).

You may be in the position to treat a very minor injury yourself, or at least get it under control before you take your bird to your avian veterinarian.

REMEMBER

Even though you'll be well equipped with your first-aid kit, it can't take the place of care by your avian veterinarian.

TIP

Your birdy first-aid kit should include:

>> Alcohol (for cleaning your tools)

>> Antibiotic ointment (a non-greasy kind, for dressing small wounds)

>> Baby bird formula (for feeding babies or weak adults)

>> Bandages and gauze (for dressing small wounds)

>> Bottled water (for cleaning eyes or wounds)

>> Cotton balls (for cleaning small wounds)

>> Dishwashing deter-gent (mild, for cleaning tools)

>> Eyedropper (for feeding weak birds)

>> Eye wash (for rinsing eyes)

>> Heating pad (for hospital cage)

>> Hydrogen peroxide (for cleaning small wounds)

>> Nail clippers (for clipping nails)

>> Nail file (for filing nails)

>> Pedialyte (to give to weak adult birds)

>> Penlight (to see better)

>> Q-Tips (for cleaning small wounds)

>> Saline solution (for rinsing small wounds or eyes)

>> Sanitary wipes (for your hands)

- » Spray bottle (for spraying solutions onto wounds or eyes)
- » Bird-safe styptic powder (to stop bleeding)
- » Syringe (without needle, for feeding weak birds)
- » Towels (small, to clean up messes)
- » Transport cage (to go to the veterinarian)
- » Tweezers (for whatever comes up)
- » Veterinarian's phone number (so you can call in an emergency)

REMEMBER

Never give your finch any over-the-counter medication meant for humans or other animals. Instead of trying to remedy the bird yourself, take it to an avian veterinarian immediately.

What to Do If Your Bird Dies

It's a sad fact that finches are quite fragile and don't have an extremely long lifespan. If you keep a small flock of finches, you will likely experience some death in your flock. If you suspect disease, your avian veterinarian can do a necropsy on the dead bird to discover what killed it (if it wasn't old age). This is important if you have other birds so that you can treat them for whatever illness the dead bird may have had.

REMEMBER

It's important that you aren't too hard on yourself when your finches die. Old age happens, illnesses happen, accidents happen. What's important is that you make every effort to keep your birds healthy and safe.

If you have a yard, you can bury your finches there and place a rock as a memorial. If you live in an apartment, perhaps there's a piece of land nearby where you can bury your little friend, or maybe you have a large potted plant where you can bury it. Your avian veterinarian can also dispose of your bird for a small fee. Nothing is stopping you from tossing the bird into the trash, but that's an undignified end to such a lovely little friend.

Chapter **9**

Breeding Your Finches

Although breeding finches can be easy — for many species, anyway — producing the best offspring can be a little more difficult. Some species are difficult to breed, and some of the more common species, such as zebras and society finches, will breed themselves to death if you let them. This chapter gives you the basics on breeding finches, if you choose to do so.

Breeding Your Finches

Breeding finches entails more than just putting two birds in a cage with a nest and hoping for the best. You must consider the processes that will keep the parents healthy so they can raise hardy chicks. These next sections detail the steps to take to ensure a productive breeding season.

Making sure you have a male and a female

This may sound like a no-brainer, but you have to start with a male and a female. Some finches — including zebras, Gouldians, and olive finches — are *dimorphic*, meaning that you can tell the males from the females. Other finches — including society finches, red-headed parrot finches, and canaries — are *monomorphic*, and you won't be able to tell the difference between the sexes by looking at them.

TIP

How can you determine which bird is male and which is female? That varies from species to species. If you purchase your finches from a breeder, they will tell you ways to determine the sex of your finches. But here are a few examples:

>> **Zebra finches:** As in many bird species, the male is more spectacular in color and patterning. He has a reddish-orange beak, as opposed to the yellowish beak of the female. He has bright patches on either side of his head, usually orange in color. He also has pronounced black and white bars on his chest, which the female doesn't have. *Remember:* This is a description of the *typical* zebra finch. Color mutations do exist, which can make sexing your birds a little more difficult.

>> **Society finches:** You won't be able to tell the difference between a male and a female society finch by looking at it. The best way to tell with a society finch is to listen for singing — only the male will sing.

>> **Gouldian finches:** The males have a brighter chest. A male has a more vivid head color than the female. In general, the male is more vivid in color and the female is more muted. Also, males sing and females do not.

>> **Whydahs:** During breeding season, the male grows a spectacular tail that is often twice the length of his body.

>> **Owl finches:** The male's breast band is thicker than in the female, and the area of white on his face is larger.

>> **Canaries:** Only the male sings. Sometimes females can have a rudimentary song, but it won't be as developed as the male's.

>> **Weavers:** The male is bright and colorful in breeding season. Outside of breeding season, he looks like a female. If you get weaver finches when the male isn't in full color, watch the birds carefully — the male weaves a nest but the female doesn't.

>> **Spice finches:** You can't tell the difference between the male and female by looking at these birds. However, the male sings a soft song and does a courtship dance to the female.

TIP

When you choose your breeding pair, make sure they get along and that they're a true pair. Watch for one bird bullying the other, quibbling between the birds, or an obvious lack of preference for each other's company. If they spend time together, share food, groom each other, and prefer to roost together for the night, the chances are excellent that you've chosen a compatible pair.

Starting with healthy birds

If you've decided to breed finches, your first priority is to ensure that your birds are in the best health possible. Don't breed while your birds are molting or ill, because this places them under considerable stress. Look for brilliant, healthy feathers, bright eyes, and a perky disposition. Look for birds that are large for their particular species. Look for clear markings and birds that stand upright and look around alertly. Avoid birds that look too thin or have drooping wings. Also, if you can buy from a breeder who has proven breeding stock and regularly shows finches, you're off to a good start. Having your veterinarian check them over before breeding is a good idea, but it isn't an absolute requirement.

REMEMBER

Make certain that the finches you choose to breed are not related. If you bought them from a breeder, they should be able to assure you of this. If you buy your birds from a pet store, you won't have any way of knowing, and the chances are that the pet store doesn't know for certain either.

TIP

Although most finches can breed as early as 3 months, do not allow them to breed until they are at least 9 months of age. For some species, breeders recommend waiting a full year. Breeding puts a tremendous amount of stress on the parents. If finches are bred too early, the offspring are often weak and sickly.

Knowing when to breed

Finches in the wild breed whenever the conditions are right. They breed when they can find sufficient quantities of water and food. Captive finches breed year-round because food, water, and a safe environment are always there for them.

WARNING

Constant breeding poses a health threat to your finches, so don't allow them to breed more than about three times per year.

Getting the right equipment

If your breeding finches are in a cage with several pairs of birds, you may witness fighting, depending on the species. Society finches, zebras, and Gouldians are usually fairly peaceful in an aviary together as long as they have enough space.

TIP

In terms of nests, most finches prefer an enclosed nest, though canaries prefer a wicker-cup nest. Bamboo finch nests are very popular, inexpensive, and easy to find. You may also be able to find a grass and twig type of nest, or a wooden box, which will work for Gouldians. Many types of nests are available, from hollow gourds to clay pots. Weaver finches prefer to weave elaborate nests of their own. Check into the needs of your species before you choose a nest.

Your breeding finches will also need a quantity of soft material to line their nest. You can buy commercial nesting material, but coming up with materials yourself is often more fun. Some ideas include shredded burlap, clean pet fur, dried grass, molted feathers, pine needles, coconut fiber, dried moss, and cotton pads.

TIP

Make sure that any nesting materials you use aren't long enough to get wrapped around a little toe, leg, or neck. Also, bamboo nests can sometimes catch a little toe in the spaces between the weaves, so make sure that both of your finches leave the nest every day.

Figuring out where to put the nest

Place the nest inside the cage as high as possible and in a corner. If you're using a wooden box, you can hang the box on the outside of the cage. Only put the nest outside of the cage if your home is free of hazards, particularly from small children or other pets. The last thing you want to do is have your finches frightened away from their nest.

Knowing what the parents need to eat

A breeding finch's diet needs protein, either from hard-boiled eggs or live insects, offered daily. Egg food is also great for nesting finches, as well as for their chicks. Calcium is also extremely important for breeding hens.

TIP

None of the foods you feed your finches should change during breeding, but the amounts — especially of calcium and proteins — should be boosted. Start to condition your birds for breeding months before you add the nest. Bulking them up before they breed is a great way of ensuring that the chicks will be healthy and the hen won't have problems laying her eggs and rearing her babies.

Prompting your finches to breed

Many finches will breed whether you want them to or not, but in the case of finches that are more difficult to breed, you need to give them some special attention to get them in the mood. Here are some things to try:

>> **Separate the male and female into separate cages within close proximity of each other.** Do this for about a week and they should miss each other so much that they'll breed soon after you reunite them.

>> **Feed lots of protein, like crushed hard-boiled egg (including the shell) and mini-mealworms.** The added protein will tell them that it's a time of abundance, and they should be prompted to breed. The extra protein will put them in good breeding condition as well.

>> **Feed egg food every day.** Egg food is very nutritious and may prompt the birds into a breeding mood.

>> **Make sure that the nest boxes are in a comfortable position for the pair — preferably high in a corner of the cage.** The pair should feel secure. The nest should be out of any bad weather, like rain, and be in a shady spot.

>> **Remove aggressive birds from the cage or aviary if they're bothering the pair.** Your pair will have trouble breeding when they're being hassled. They may not breed at all or may abandon eggs or babies. Also, another aggressive bird can kill one of the pair.

>> **Offer a steady source of calcium, such as a cuttlebone.** Breeding hens need extra calcium to aid in egg production. Calcium will leach from her bones if she doesn't have enough in her diet; this can cause tremendous health problems, including egg binding, and even death.

>> **Offer a variety of nesting materials.** Every finch pair is different in the materials they prefer. When they find the materials they like, they'll begin to line their nest.

>> **Be sure they have clean, fresh drinking and bathing water.** This is true for any bird, breeding or not. Water is another sign of abundance, putting the pair at ease to breed.

>> **Make sure that the pair is undisturbed.** Too much noise or activity near the cage or nest can disrupt breeding or rearing of the babies.

>> **Clean the nest between each *clutch* (group of eggs and/or babies).** The nest will be soiled after each successful breeding. You may want to replace the nest with a new one.

Understanding the incubation period

Finches normally share the incubation period, with both the male and the female taking turns sitting in the nest and keeping the eggs warm. Because most finch nests have a cover, telling when your hen starts to lay may be difficult.

Typically, the hen will lay one egg per day until she's finished. Finches average between one and six eggs in a *clutch* (a group of babies). The hen will become more and more reluctant to leave the nest, but the male will spend part of the day incubating the eggs and give her a break for food and movement. She will also bathe and bring the moisture back to her eggs.

The incubation period for finches ranges from 12 days for some of the waxbills, to 13 days for zebras, to 15 days for Gouldians. If you can, peek inside the nest when the parents are out of it. Leave them alone as much as possible, but try to peek at least once a day after she's done laying all the eggs. If a week goes by and the eggs don't change color a little — usually turning grayish or growing darker —chances are that the eggs aren't fertile and will not produce babies.

TIP

If you want to know for sure whether the eggs are fertile, you can buy a *candler,* which is a little flashlight with a long wand at the end. Place the end of the wand gently on the egg. If the egg is fertile, you'll see veins and the outline of an embryo. This is called *candling* the egg, and it's a common practice among breeders.

Don't panic if you can't see the eggs at first glance. Finches commonly cover the eggs with a bit of nesting material to help keep them warm. However, if they bury the eggs too deeply, the chicks will die when they hatch. This is why keeping an eye on the nest is a good idea.

TIP

Occasionally, you'll have fertile eggs that don't hatch. Often, the parents leave the nest for too long and allow the eggs to become cold. If they're nervous, they may stay out of the nest. It's important for the parent finches to have peace and quiet during this period. Disturb them only to supply them with food and water.

The eggs will hatch one per day, in the order in which they were laid. The hatchlings don't look much like birds at all. A few species have little bits of fluff on them, but they don't really have down yet. If you look closely at them, you'll actually be able to see food in their crops if the parents are feeding them. Making sure right away that they're being fed is important.

Many people are frightened because the crop on a new hatchling appears grotesquely swollen with food. This is not a problem. It means that your finches are feeding the hatchlings well. If the crop becomes too full, the hatchling cannot raise its head and ask for more until the food digests a bit — the baby bird won't explode, despite appearances.

Around three weeks the babies will start to leave the nest. By six weeks or so they will look like adults. This is the time to separate them from their parents — unless the parents have already gone to nest again, in which case, you'll want to separate them sooner.

Feeding and weaning chicks

Parent birds eat the foods you offer and then regurgitate the partially digested food into the mouths of the babies. Often, the male will eat and then return to the nest and regurgitate food into the mouth of the hen, who then will regurgitate that food into the open beaks of the chicks. This is why the food you provide must be very nutritious.

The parent birds will be responsible for weaning the chicks onto adult food. Babies begin to leave the nest at around three weeks (depending on species) and will start to explore their environment. During weaning, the babies will leave the nest for longer periods and mimic the parents' behaviors. Provide millet spray, veggies, egg food, soft whole-wheat bread, and small live insects, such as grubs and mini-mealworms. The babies will wean onto soft foods before they begin to tackle eating hard foods, like hulling mature seeds.

Knowing What to Do When Something Goes Wrong

A number of things can go wrong when your birds breed. The first problem, which is the most minor as well as the most obvious, is that your breeding pair may not like each other. In that case, rearrange your birds and try again. Here are a few more issues to consider.

Egg binding

The next most likely thing to go wrong is *egg binding,* which is when the female cannot pass her egg. A swollen abdomen may be a sign of egg binding in a female finch. If a hen is not well nourished, especially if she hasn't gotten enough calcium in her diet, her eggs may have soft shells, which will make the eggs difficult to lay, resulting in egg binding. Egg binding can also occur when the egg is malformed, or when the bird has a tumor or some other disorder of the reproductive system. Symptoms of egg binding include panting, lameness (inability to use her legs), and puffiness. Consult your veterinarian immediately if you suspect this problem.

Normally, an egg is passed within a day of noticeable swelling. If you notice your hen having serious troubles and it's the middle of the night or if you can't get to your avian veterinarian right away, move her to a warm (85° F to 90° F, or 29° C to 32° C) and humid hospital cage.

Making a hospital cage is easy. You'll need a 10-gallon aquarium or a plastic animal keeper, an aquarium thermometer, a heating pad, a screen or a plastic-vented top for the aquarium, paper towels, and a towel. Put the heating pad on the medium setting and place it underneath one-half of the aquarium. Place a few layers of paper towels on the bottom of the aquarium. Make sure to put shallow dishes of food and water in the aquarium, too — make sure the water is very shallow, because a weak bird can drown in water as deep as one inch. Place the bird in the aquarium; then cover the aquarium with the screen top. Cover the aquarium three-fourths of the way with a dark towel. The bird should be able to move away from the heat if she wants to. Make sure that the temperature in the tank stays at about 98° F to 99° F (about 37° C).

Gently put a small drop of mineral oil or olive oil in her beak with an eyedropper and place a few drops of the same in her vent (where the egg comes out). This may help her to pass the egg.

Even if she does pass the egg, take her to the veterinarian as soon as you can. If your hen survives, don't breed her again until she is fully recovered and you've boosted her calcium and nutrient intake.

Infertile eggs

The first eggs that your hen lays may not be fertile — not a major problem. Wait 21 days to be certain that the eggs won't hatch, and then remove the eggs. You can leave the nest and nesting material intact. Your hen should begin laying again immediately. If you don't want her to lay again, simply remove the nest.

Inexperienced parent birds

Some parents don't feed their first clutch, but they usually get the idea by the second clutch. If you notice that the parents aren't feeding their babies, you can foster them under society finches that also have babies (put them in the society's nest), or finches of the same species that have proven themselves to be good parents. If you can't do this, you can try to handfeed them yourself (more on that later in this chapter).

REMEMBER

In the early days of your hatchlings' lives, you need to ensure that the parents are still fed as well as they were in the days leading up to the hatching. Remember that the male finch may be eating for as many as eight mouths (sometimes including the hen). So even if he's the only one you see eating, keep the groceries coming.

Tossing the chicks

Tossing is a particularly ugly problem. Once in a while, one of the parents simply tosses a chick out of the nest. Gouldians do this often, but any species may exhibit the behavior now and then. Possible causes include a finch that simply doesn't know what to do with a wiggling baby, or parents rattled by too much commotion nearby or by intrusive checking of the nest. You may have a bird that habitually tosses the babies out of the nest.

If you find a tossed baby, place it gently back into the nest. It's possible that the baby simply fell out. Check to see whether the parents are feeding it. If not, or if the baby has been tossed again, you'll need to intervene.

The best way to help a tossed baby is either to foster the chick (or chicks) with another set of parents or to handfeed the baby yourself (see information about both later in this chapter).

HELPING YOUR FINCH SURVIVE THE LOSS OF A MATE

Although finches are not always monogamous, they do prefer to pair with another finch for life. When one of two paired birds dies, from illness or any other cause, it is terribly stressful for the survivor. If the mate's death was not due to illness, you may want to introduce another bird as a companion right away. Place the new finch in a cage next to the existing finch and allow them to get to know each other for a few days. If they seem to get along, you can add the existing finch to the new finch's cage.

If the hen died during incubating or rearing chicks, foster or handfeed the chicks right away. Sometimes the male will take up rearing duties. Keep an eye on the babies to make sure they're being fed.

Failure to thrive

In some cases, chicks simply don't thrive. They lose weight and die before reaching adulthood. In many cases, this is due to inbreeding, so be sure not to breed that particular pair again. Now and then, a bacterial or fungal infection too mild to trouble the adults can cause death for the chicks. The only person who can determine this is your veterinarian. Have the doctor examine the body of any chick who doesn't survive.

REMEMBER

If your chicks survive the first three days, they'll probably make it.

Finding foster parents for your babies

Sometimes parent finches will toss their chicks or won't feed them, so you'll need to find foster parents. Zebra finches and society finches are very good foster parents. The foster parents don't need to be of the same species as the hatchlings, although feeding the foster parents a diet close to the natural diet of the fostered chicks is a good idea. Contrary to the myths surrounding fostering, the babies will grow up to be full-fledged members of their own species, and they won't exhibit the behaviors of their foster parents when they grow to adulthood.

REMEMBER

Choose a species known for successful fostering. Society finches seem to be the best foster parents, with zebras running a close second. Choose foster parents that have unflappable temperaments. If you're fostering eggs that have been abandoned, be certain that the foster parents don't see you add the eggs to their nest. Fostering is always a throw of the dice, but it's worth trying.

Another reason to have a good set of foster parents is if you have a finch pair that are too prolific. Finches can easily raise three to five babies, but after five, it may be difficult for them, and the younger babies may die. Remember, a week-old finch is far larger and stronger than a hatchling. If you notice six to eight eggs, or more, you may want to try to put the newer eggs into the nest of a foster pair if you have them.

Handfeeding baby finches

Sometimes a nestling gets tossed and you don't have other finch parents to raise it. In this case, you'll have to take on the duties of raising the baby yourself. It's tricky because these birds are so small, but don't be daunted – you can do it in an emergency. (See Figure 9-1.)

REMEMBER

Never remove babies from successful finch parents. This can cause great distress and long-term effects for both parents and babies. You'll only handfeed babies that need it.

First, place the babies into a nest like they would be with their parents. Next, you'll need an incubator/brooder. You can purchase one at a feed store or online. In a pinch, you can create a brooder the same way you create a hospital cage. You'll place the nest into the brooder.

Keep new babies at a consistent temperature of 92° F to 94° F Fahrenheit (33.3° C to 34.4° C). Each week you can lower the temperature a few degrees. By the time the babies are fully feathered and weaned, they can be at room temperature.

FIGURE 9-1:
This zebra
finch
nestling
may need
to be
handfed if
its parents
have
abandoned
it.

kurashova / 123 RF

You'll need commercially prepared handfeeding formula and a small pipette or syringe. The babies will need to be fed every hour around the clock when they are young. As they get older, they can be fed every two hours, every three hours, and then just during the day.

Always use fresh formula and clean, sterilized feeding utensils. Make sure the formula isn't too hot and, if you microwave it, be sure to stir very well to avoid hot areas in the formula. Don't over-feed or risk aspirating (choking) the chicks to death. Don't under-feed either. The process is fairly intense and has a steep learning curve, so please look online for video tutorials on how to handfeed baby finches properly. Hopefully you'll never have to do it.

Finding good homes for your baby finches

Finding homes for your baby finches could prove to be your biggest problem. Letting the little ones go can be difficult. Wait until your birds are completely weaned before you re-home them. Eight weeks or more is ideal.

If you take your baby finches to a pet shop, there is a chance that they won't go to good homes. In fact, some people feed inexpensive finches to their larger birds, such as toucans.

TIP

Giving them away may help you find the most homes in the shortest period, but try to sell them for a reasonable price if you can. When you charge a fair price for your finches, you may be more likely to find people who take the responsibility seriously.

Discouraging Breeding

Most finches will take a break from breeding when you remove the nest from the cage, but some pairs are determined and will lay eggs in feed cups and on the bottom of the cage. Here are a few things you can do to help prevent breeding:

>> **Remove the nest and all nesting materials:** If they have nowhere to nest, they may stop. But this won't stop a determined pair. Change feeders to tube style, so they can't nest in their feed cups.

>> **Separate the sexes:** You can separate the males from the females if you truly don't want more babies, but realize that they mate for life and will be lonely without each other.

>> **Start a scarcity diet:** To bring birds into breeding condition you have to simulate the spring, when food is bountiful. Simulating scarcity may give them the notion that it's not time to breed. Cut back (but do not completely eliminate) egg food, protein, and live foods, like worms.

>> **Buy dummy eggs:** If your finches have started a nest and you didn't catch it in time, you can remove their eggs and replace them with plastic dummy eggs that you can purchase online.

>> **Reduce daylight:** If your finches are indoors, you can reduce the amount of light that they receive to 9 or 10 hours a day. This way, they will think that the time of bounty is over and that winter is coming — that's not typically breeding season for them.

The Part of Tens

Finding the best finch websites

Creating DIY toys for your finches

Chapter **10**
Ten Great Finch Websites

» **Finch Information Center:** `http://www.finchinfo.com/index.php:` This site has helpful information about all types of finches and their care. You'll find photos and informative articles.

» **National Finch and Softbill Society:** `www.nfss.org:` Founded in 1984, the National Finch and Softbill Society is devoted to all types of finches. Here you'll find dozens of articles on finch care and breeding, as well as a section for photos of members' birds.

» **HotSpot for Birds:** `www.multiscope.com/hotspot:` This site offers many articles about all types of birds, including finches, and contains a great deal of information about bird safety. It sells products as well.

» **Canary and Finch Society:** `https://www.canaryandfinchsociety.com:` A not-for-profit club that promotes education about all birds with an emphasis on finches and canaries.

>> **Finch Forum:** `https://www.finchforum.com`: This finch forum is for beginners and experts alike and will help you connect with other finch lovers.

>> **The Finch Farm:** `https://thefinchfarm.com`: This site offers a huge variety of finches for sale, along with a lot of good information about their care.

>> **EBird:** `https://ebird.org/home`: This site from the Cornell Lab of Ornithology has lots of detailed finch information. You'll find excellent photos and detailed descriptions of finch species.

>> **Ray Brown's Talkin' Birds:** `https://www.talkinbirds.com`: The companion site to an all-bird podcast.

>> **Save the Gouldian Fund:** `https://savethegouldian.net`: A non-profit organization dedicated to saving the wild Gouldian finch. Lots of great photos and info.

>> **National Audubon Society:** `https://www.audubon.org`: An all-bird site with a lot of information about finches from all over the world.

Chapter **11**

Ten Fun DIY Toys for Finches

>> **Fun with string.** Tie some sisal or jute twine around a perch and onto the cage bars and watch your finches have fun unraveling the twine. Watch to ensure that any loose threads don't get caught around a neck or foot.

>> **Shredded paper.** Paper shreds are fun for your finches to play with. Make sure the paper is free of ink and dyes. Brown crimped packing paper is great.

>> **Playing with Popsicle sticks.** Using only nontoxic white school glue or paste, you can create ladder, swings, perches, and other fun items for your finches. Remember, only use nontoxic glue that a preschooler would use (and perhaps eat).

>> **Foraging toys.** Finches in the wild forage for their food. You can create foraging toys by placing some of their favorite food into white tissue paper, crumpling it slightly, then placing it at the bottom of the cage. Sprinkle some of their food on top so they get the idea to investigate.

>> **Toilet paper rolls.** Save your cardboard toilet paper rolls and place them at the bottom of the cage to give your finches something to investigate. If you're worried about bacteria on the rolls, pass them under a UV light or run a hair dryer on the hottest setting over them before giving them to your finches.

>> **Hangers.** If your finches' housing is large enough, hang a wooden clothes hanger from the top of the housing and watch your little ones swing away! If the perch area of the hanger is too slick, wrap it with some sisal or jute twine. You can also use the twine to tie some plastic buttons at the top of the hanger to dangle near the perch.

>> **Straws.** Paper straws can become fun foraging toys. Tie a bundle of straw together at the center using a zip tie. Next, fill the straws with seeds, egg food, and other goodies. Hang it in the cage and watch your finches forage.

>> **DIY treat sticks.** Coat Popsicle sticks in a thin layer of organic peanut butter (the only ingredient should be peanuts). Dip the coated stick in egg food. Allow to dry overnight (or longer) and weave it between the bars of the cage or stick it straight up into the feed dish. Keep unused sticks in freezer until you're ready to offer to your finches.

>> **Willow balls.** You can purchase small willow balls online and then fill them with food to create a fun foraging toy. Hang in the cage with twine or a pipe cleaner, or just place it on the bottom of the cage.

>> **Pom-poms.** Small, colorful, puffy pom-poms from the craft store make fun exploration toys for finches. They may even take them back to their nests.

Index

About the Author

Nikki Moustaki, M.A., M.F.A., is an avian care and behavior consultant and the author of more than 30 books on birds and bird behavior. She is also the author of the bird-related memoir, *The Bird Market of Paris*. She has kept and/or bred lovebirds, cockatiels, budgies (parakeets), lories, macaws, amazons, conures, finches, canaries, ringnecks, and brotergeris. She advocates for responsible bird care and encourages everyone to participate in avian rescue efforts.

Dedication

You have no idea how high I can fly.

Author's Acknowledgments

I would like to thank everyone who made this book possible, including Kelsey Baird, Christopher Morris, Michelle Hacker, and Mohammed Zafar Ali.

Publisher's Acknowledgments

Acquisitions Editor: Kelsey Baird

Project Editor: Christopher Morris

Copy Editor: Christopher Morris

Technical Editor: Becky Margison

Production Editor:
Mohammed Zafar Ali

Cover Image: © David Pegzlz/
Shutterstock